W9-CBB-963

DATE DUE

Praise for *The 12 Factors of Business Success*

"Kevin Hogan is a thinker—and a doer. He has a devoted following that lives by his wisdom. His latest book on achievement is not optional. If you are looking to climb the success ladder, Kevin Hogan's book will be there for you at every rung of the journey—to teach you, to support you, and to encourage you to achieve your dreams."

—Jeffrey Gitomer, author of *The Little Red Book of Selling*

"One of the most intelligent and genuinely thoughtful books written on the subject of success."

—Mark Joyner, futurist and #1 best-selling author of *Simpleology*

"The authors' valuable insights on business success and leadership will help people in any walk of life take their performance to the next level. *The 12 Factors of Business Success* is an impressive, straightforward, no-nonsense road map to bring out the best in each one of us."

—Steven McWhorter, CEO, Securities America, Inc.

"Mollie Marti is a wise success coach with a personal commitment to excellence and a passion for helping others produce results consistent with their values and aspirations. Her collaboration with Hogan and Lakhani has resulted in a powerful, practical, and fun guide to getting the most out of your business and life."

—Michael Port, author of *Book Yourself Solid* and
Beyond Booked Solid

"Mollie Marti inspires excellence while providing down-to-earth, useful ideas and tools for success. This collaboration with two other premier coaches gives readers a smart and savvy plan to master the battle zone of everyday business."

—Dale Collie, former U.S. Army Ranger; author of
Winning Under Fire, Building Courageous Leaders,
and *Frontline Leadership*

THE 12 factors of BUSINESS SUCCESS

THE 12 factors of BUSINESS SUCCESS

DISCOVER, DEVELOP, AND LEVERAGE YOUR STRENGTHS

KEVIN HOGAN, DAVE LAKHANI, MOLLIE MARTI

WILEY

John Wiley & Sons, Inc.

Published by John Wiley & Sons, Inc., Hoboken, New Jersey.
Published simultaneously in Canada.

Limit of Liability/Disclaimer of Warranty: While the publisher and author have used their best efforts in preparing this book, they make no representations or warranties with respect to the accuracy or completeness of the contents of this book and specifically disclaim any implied warranties of merchantability or fitness for a particular purpose. No warranty may be created or extended by sales representatives or written sales materials. The advice and strategies contained herein may not be suitable for your situation. You should consult with a professional where appropriate. Neither the publisher nor author shall be liable for any loss of profit or any other commercial damages, including but not limited to special, incidental, consequential, or other damages.

For general information on our other products and services or for technical support, please contact our Customer Care Department within the United States at (800) 762-2974, outside the United States at (317) 572-3993 or fax (317) 572-4002.

Wiley also publishes its books in a variety of electronic formats. Some content that appears in print may not be available in electronic books. For more information about Wiley products, visit our web site at www.wiley.com.

Library of Congress Cataloging-in-Publication Data:

Hogan, Kevin.
The 12 factors of business success : discover, develop, and leverage your strengths / Kevin Hogan, Dave Lakhani, Mollie Marti.
    p.   cm.
    Includes bibliographical references and index.
    ISBN 978-0-470-29299-0 (cloth)
    1. Success in business.   I. Lakhani, Dave, 1965–.   II. Marti, Mollie Weighner.
  III. Title.   IV. Title: Twelve factors of business success.
  HF5386.H653 2008
  650.1—dc22   2008012236

Printed in the United States of America.

10 9 8 7 6 5 4 3 2 1

Kevin Hogan:

To Katie, Jessica, and Mark Hogan

Dave Lakhani:

To Stephanie and Austria, both a key to and an example of my success.

And to you, for embracing my work; thank you.

Mollie Marti:

To Monte, Nathaniel, Alaina, and Erin. If something doesn't work for us, it doesn't work for me. Thanks for making this project work.

Contents

Foreword

by Mark Joyner, Founder of Simpleology

Do we really need another book about business success?

Well, if you look at all that's been written and read on the subject, and compare that to the average Joe's lot in life, apparently the answer is yes.

When I first set out to write this Foreword I was pre-penning in my mind something trite: "Look, the message of success has been said again and again in different ways, but it hasn't changed. You just need to keep hearing it in different ways until you get it."

Nonsense.

The fact of the matter is, much of the success literature of the past 100 years is utter rubbish.

Much of it is written by people who have never accomplished a thing in their lives. They get the notion that "people who make and sell business success tools make lots of money, and so should I," and thus it begins.

So, keep that in mind when you read supposedly authoritative books on success. It's easier than you think to create the appearance of authority.

Rather than rehash the easy (and sometimes downright untrue) messages of the self-help industry and call them their own, the three coauthors of this book have instead chosen to do something far more valuable: They asked about each of these notions, "Is that *really* true?"

It's not easy to challenge assumptions—especially popular ones.

Yet, the lasting accomplishments of history have rarely come from those who have set out to do easy things.

Actually, back up a minute.

Did you accept that last statement as true?

It sure sounds nice, but is it *really* true?

I have no idea. It just came out in the flow of writing, and after I wrote it I paused for a second and questioned it myself. I was about to delete it and thought instead I should leave it as an example for you.

Bullshit sometimes comes wrapped in a very pretty package.

It's possible that a great many marvelous accomplishments have been achieved by those who set out to do the easy thing. (That's a nonsense statement, and I can't imagine how I could evaluate its truth one way or another.)

This book attempts to strip back that pretty package and ask what's really inside the box. What you find may in fact surprise you.

Preface

Everyone wants to achieve.

We all want to be good at something.

Some of us want to become good at a lot of things.

We all want to be happy and successful.

We use the word "success" a lot in this book. What does this word mean? For us, we define success simply as achieving whatever it is that you've set out to do in your life. It is the mental state that allows you to accomplish your goals and live your life to your fullest ability and capacity. The definition of success is purely individual and measured by you.

How do you define success? If you don't already have a clear answer to that question, you will by the time you are done reading this book.

When you gain clarity about where you want to go and you change a few flawed persistent thoughts that many people hold onto and make a few steps in the right direction amazing things can happen.

This book is going to be different, very different, from many things you've been told or taught about success and achievement.

While we uncover the 12 Factors of Business Success, we will also remove the myths and folklore about success. We will show you what really drives the best to the top. We also will give you concrete success actions that *really* work. You will learn how to discover, develop, and leverage your strengths and take your success to a whole new level.

Each of us does high-level coaching and consulting in addition to presenting to audiences around the world. That means we get to watch the successful become even more successful and those who have decided to move beyond mediocrity succeed.

We listened as our clients asked questions in person and by e-mail. We include some of these questions in this book with answers that we carefully and thoroughly crafted to give the most up-to-the-minute information about what works in the real world. The real world where you will succeed or fail every day. We believe that many of your questions will be answered in this book. Questions you've asked the wall, the chair, and your cup of coffee many times.

And there is more.

Each of us is a meticulous student. Our opinions are like the opinions of all of the most successful people on this planet. When presented with new information that is better than the old, we're happy to replace one for the other if need be. We aren't married to any ideas herein. These are simply the facts and factors of achievement as they have been studied, researched, refined and proven.

There are a number of characteristics and skills that people must cultivate and develop in their lives before they can become successful in whatever path they choose. These traits, including being disciplined, taking the right kind of action, making decisions, creating passion, and being confident are the building blocks of achievement. We look closely at each of these foundational skills as well as the more advanced skills needed to build success in business and in life, including mastering criticism, exercising self-control, strengthening resiliency, building wealth, and putting support structures in place. We conclude with a comprehensive chapter on the Success Mind and an inside look at how high achievers really think and view the world.

You can build a life without these business success skills. But like building a house without a strong foundation, it'll be put at risk with the first heavy wind or rainstorm. And you don't need to be told that life will have a few more of those.

The Genesis of Success: Intention versus Behavior

The Christmas present didn't fit. There were no batteries in the gift for the boy. The food wasn't quite as good as you wanted it to be for the occasion. But no one cared all that much because your intention was good.

In areas of kindness and concern, intention goes a long way even if things go wrong. But intention is just that. It's part of the plan. Some people's plan is a hope. I "hope things work out." Success requires more.

Achievement begins with intention. Intention happens on day one. That's today. And today it is very important. But over time, the intention rarely matters.

We know that when observing the actual behaviors of people vs. their attitudes we see big differences. We've learned to watch what people do and not what they say. Achievement goes beyond intention and requires action. Real action.

Success and achievement are in large part processes that begin and end in your own mind. While your actions and outer circumstances obviously have a huge impact on your success, achievement is not so much about what you do, but how you do it.

How do you do what you do every day? If you change your actions, you will change your results. If you change your thoughts, you will change your results. Change both thoughts and actions and achieving most things is within reach of most people. We've seen it happen again and again. And now it's your turn.

This book takes you from *wanting* to be a top performer to *behaving* your way to success. It's quite a ride and there's no better time to begin. Let's get started.

Acknowledgments

Kevin Hogan

Special thanks are in order for Matt Holt, our editor at Wiley.

Writing a book always takes you away from the people who want to be in your space the most. So for Katie, Mark, and Jessica, thank you for putting up with #18.

Michelle Drum, Jennifer Battaglino, Lisa McLellan, Ken Owens, and Mark Ryan all make my life better and are often sources of ideas and support. Thanks guys.

A special tip of the hat to my dear friends Scott and Carmen Schluter and Devin and Rachel Hastings.

And of course to my co-authors without whom this book would have been much shorter—they are fabulous!

Dave Lakhani

I'd like to thank every person who has ever listened to me speak and who has been moved to action. The thousands of letters, e-mails, and phone calls I get every year makes writing books like this a joy.

I'd also like to thank Matt Holt whose great insights and willingness to take chances makes writing for him a joy.

Kevin and Mollie, writing with you has been an exceptional experience. You've both challenged me to be a better writer and to dig deeper and share more. You are both an inspiration to me.

Finally, no acknowledgment would ever be complete without thanking my wife and daughter who exemplify one of my core beliefs about success. Without their support success wouldn't be nearly as sweet.

Mollie Marti

My gratitude starts with Monte, Nate, Alaina, and Erin, who truly get my need to write and do the work I do. You know I've got your back as you pursue your own passions. Your dreams are my dreams.

Thanks to my 12 amazing brothers and sisters. Spending time with you always feels like coming home. And to Harold and Shirley Marti, who love me like a daughter.

Thank you to my extraordinary clients, who provide me with precious opportunities to work with, witness, and be inspired by stars striving to live their best life. A special acknowledgment to Leah Badertscher, Patty Kuehn, and Sheila Deininger, who provide great moral support and wise feedback on whatever project I throw myself into.

Thank you to Matt Holt, our wonderful editor, and to Linda Charbonneau for her fabulous administrative support.

And heartfelt gratitude to Kevin Hogan and Dave Lakhani, from whom the lessons and support have never ceased since the moment they came into my life. Thanks, guys!

1

Self-Discipline

Self-discipline is the rejection of instant gratification in favor of something better. It is the giving up of instant pleasure and satisfaction for a good opportunity or reward that is far more important and valuable in the future. It is the ability to go through the rigor of repeating an activity again and again until your skill or competence increases.

Self-discipline was once the core characteristic of an American. It remained so for 300 years. But now it is becoming a bit of a rare commodity. Losing that one trait will change the fate of a person or a nation.

The reality is that most people do not master self-discipline. This is true even when faced with a need to create massive change or to follow a strict course of action with a consequence of dying if one does not become disciplined. This phenomenon has been studied over and over again with the same results. Even people who face death if they do not make substantial changes in their lifestyles often fail to make the necessary changes. For instance, Dr. Edward Miller, the dean of the medical school and CEO of the hospital at Johns Hopkins University, observed, "If you look at people after coronary artery bypass grafting two years later, 90 percent of them have not changed their lifestyle." (Deutschman 2007). It is not an exaggeration to say that the quality of your life and health rely on self-discipline.

The achievement of your dreams and goals also relies on your ability to master this critical component of success. If you want to develop the ability to create long-term and replicable success you must develop discipline. That means that whatever you have to do in order to increase your skill or competence and achieve results needs to be repeated again and again. You must discipline yourself (or others) with intention and effort until the behaviors manifest and become self-perpetuating.

Did you go to the grocery store this week and get food?

In all likelihood someone in your home goes shopping every week. Let's say it's you. If you do it, you eat. If you don't, then you pay a price. You go instead of watching TV or sleeping or reading the comics. Why? Well, you just do.

And that's how it must be. If you want to eat you simply have little alternative but to go. You intentionally manifest the behavior of getting up, getting into the car, and going shopping until it becomes a habit and something you no longer think about. It's now a normal part of your routine.

Self-discipline drives success. You must repeat the target behavior, whatever it is, every day until it becomes second nature. Until it becomes a habit. Automatic. It is about behaving your way to success.

What is the attitude of the person with self-discipline? "I am in charge of my behavior." Self-discipline is the attitude of achievement. "I do it every day. I control my behavior. I decide what I want in my life. I run my life." You become your behavior not your intentions and by doing so become not only a better human being but a higher achiever.

Self-discipline is one of the most critical aspects of achievement that we will talk about. It is a building block that we will add to. It certainly is not the beginning and the end. You can have self-discipline and fail. You can make it harder to be disciplined because you lack emotion or a deeper understanding of why you do what you do. You can have self-discipline and never do anything that matters. Those are all possible results. But, without self-discipline there is no achievement. There is no success.

You can win a game without self-discipline. You can't win a Super Bowl, the World Series, or the World Cup without it.

Self-discipline is best wrapped up in one word: "Until." You simply do whatever it is *until* it is done.

Perseverance and renewing genesis are important components of self-discipline.

Perseverance is the driving factor of self-discipline. To persevere means to refuse to stop. It means to maintain a state of unbending and unyielding movement toward an outcome. If you don't give up at something you attempt, then you can't fail. If something doesn't work out as planned the first time, then you must try and try again using different methods to achieve the result that you are looking for.

Perseverance requires placing thought (objective analysis of what needs to be done) over feelings (I'm tired). You must learn to follow your thoughts instead of your feelings. You master your feelings and manifest your thoughts. You will achieve at a higher level if you develop a strong awareness of what your feelings are doing to your actions and if you can move when your body asks you to be inert.

Renewing genesis means beginning each day or each part of the day without having to think about pursuing your goal. You simply begin again where you left off. Yesterday you wrote pages

248 to 254 in your new book. Today you write 255 to 261. It makes no difference what else is on your to-do list or what comes up during the day. You decide to do it and then you do it until it's done.

You never allow yourself to think, "I wonder if I should ... today." That sentence leads to eternal failure. When do you find the time? You prioritize it. You get it done. Everything else comes next.

You *do*, because you decided you would. You trust yourself and you teach yourself that you are worthy of trust by doing what you decide to do.

This is so important to understand: If you can't rely on yourself to follow through on your own decisions ... if you can't trust yourself to follow through, then you will fail. You can have all the positive attitude on the planet and never move. Without decisions and follow-through, you fail. Those who don't ever decide and discipline themselves to carry through on their decisions cannot achieve at a high level.

Decision followed by action creates self trust. When you create self trust, others begin to trust you and want to be around you because you make things happen. You begin to build momentum toward greater success.

Decide and do until.

Question: I'm an idea person and a great starter. I get big and promising ideas and start taking action toward implementing them. But then I usually get so excited by my next great idea that I'm off chasing that before I finish the one I was working on. What is the secret to finishing a job?

One common reason people don't stick with something until it is done is that they don't believe they actually can finish it. People won't persevere or give their best effort if they don't believe that they are capable of achieving more. Does this describe you?

Do you think that if a task requires too much effort it won't be worth it?

Do you consistently avoid working any harder than you have to?

Do you believe that massive success is only for the truly talented and lucky, so there's no point in giving your best?

It sounds like you (in the company of most people) are capable of several times more than you have achieved so far. Do you have trouble believing that, or do you feel a twinge in your gut that confirms the truth of that statement? If you really don't believe you are capable of more, then you are already working at your current maximum level of excellence. However, if you are willing to just consider that you're capable of more, you are in the right mind-set to change your life.

Research shows that people perform better when they believe they can perform better and when they believe they are in control of their performance. The first step is a willingness to just consider that you're capable of more.

Take a moment to think about your accomplishments thus far, and be honest with yourself about the things you could have done better. You fail to finish things. What else is there? Perhaps you shied away from increased responsibility at your job and got passed over for a promotion or you gave up on making your dream a reality because it seemed too difficult.

In order to change your behavior, you need to first acknowledge that your current circumstances are generally due to the actions you've taken so far, and more importantly the quality and intensity of effort you've put forth. Imagine you're in a shopping mall, standing before one of those maps that state, "You are here." If you know where you are, you can easily map out a route to get somewhere else.

It is important not to judge yourself too harshly for your lack of accomplishment up to this point. For some people, feelings of guilt can cause them to move more decisively and take measured and focused action. But for many, these negative feelings accomplish nothing.

The point is to gain a clear understanding of where you are and figure out where you want to go. Acknowledge that you did the best you could with the resources you had, but now you are ready to do better and be more.

This can be an uncomfortable exercise because in a sense it means acknowledging that you are the cause of your own stunted progress. However, only by knowing with certainty where you *are* can you move on to somewhere *better.*

Success Actions That Work: This chapter is the starting place for you. Self-discipline. You need to act your way to success. You need to overwrite some dominant bad habits.

You have formed a habit of starting and not finishing things. No matter how fired up you get about the latest project, your old, ingrained habits are as solid as concrete. The biggest mistakes people make are often in underestimating the amount of energy that will be required when they first start making changes.

Doing that which you are familiar with takes little new energy and is rarely overridden by anything else. We're used to doing things a certain way and if we try to change those comfortable old routines, we feel nervous and out of place.

In order to become comfortable with a new habit of finishing, you need to stick with it long enough so that it becomes second nature. That's a lot easier said than done. Remember, that's how you got comfortable where you are—even if it's not exactly where you want to be.

You will increase your chances for real and lasting change by seeking out a mentor or working with a coach. Most successful people have coaches and mentors to help them along the way because some things in the equation of achievement simply meet with a lot of inertia. These support people can help make sure you stick with it until you get to the point where you don't need that extra boost each week.

A significant amount of action, focus, and will is needed in order to change old habits. The good news is that once changed, like cement, they become unconscious and semipermanent.

Question: **For how long do you persist? I read that successful people never give up. I've also read that sometimes you shouldn't beat your head against the wall expecting a different result (a definition of insanity). If you're not succeeding, how do you know when to quit?**

The advice does appear to be in conflict. One person says persist until you succeed. Another person says to give up the sinking ship. The point being that once you've tried something and it doesn't work, it's time to move on to something that does. Your confusion is completely understandable, especially coming from the point of frustration in which you find yourself after hitting the proverbial brick wall.

The short answer is that you quit when you stop believing in what you are doing.

The longer answer is that you have to carefully evaluate what you've done to succeed. Chances are high that you've done a lot of busy work and talking but not taken a lot of action. You have to carefully decide if you are not succeeding because something isn't possible for you or if you've not succeeded because you haven't put in the hard work it takes to succeed. If you really want to achieve something and you haven't tried every possible avenue to success, then don't give up. If you've exhausted every possibility available to you and you are still not getting a result and your belief is that you won't, it may be time to stop.

The other time to quit is when the goal is rendered no longer valid or useful. As you progress through a series of goals you may realize that one of your goals that you've worked hard on was misguided. The time to stop is the moment you recognize your error. Don't give it any more time or effort. Put that energy toward another more meaningful goal.

Perhaps an example from one author's personal history would be helpful. Here is Kevin's experience when submitting one of his early books for publication:

I submitted the book *The Psychology of Persuasion* 247 times to 247 different publishers before it was accepted by Pelican Publishing. Even then, it was obvious that they barely believed the book (and the author promoting the book) would sell.

In retrospect, I couldn't blame any of the 247 publishers. They had no logical reason to believe the book would sell. None. I had written two books. Both were self-published with fewer than 1,000 sales each. That's not much of a track record.

One well-known publisher clearly told me the book was poorly written and the subject matter was marginal. Whew.

Today, next to Zig Ziglar's *See You at the Top,* I believe *The Psychology of Persuasion* is Pelican's best-selling book. Internationally, approximately one million copies have sold. There are a lot of books that sell better, but the point is that the book has done quite well.

So should I have quit and done something else?

The answer didn't exist within the track record. It was to be found in personal drive. I had predetermined that I would make the book successful. I wanted the book published, I wanted it to sell well, and that meant I would go above and beyond the call of any duty to sell the book. I would do radio shows in the middle of the night, speak to groups as small as five or six people, do book signings where only one or two or no one showed up.

Because I had predetermined that as my outcome, the book would sell. I didn't just know it or get a feeling about it. I was going to make it happen every day. The work involved during the first few years was overwhelming. But I made it happen.

I persisted until I succeeded. All of that said, I probably would have suggested to 98 percent of people I've coached that they move along after about 100 rejections.

The book became symbolic of me as a person and I wasn't going to have me thrown aside. I and my book were going to succeed on some level.

Success Actions That Work: The answer to whether you continue to persist or choose to move on really is a question rooted in utility and decision making. If you are going to go with the flow and see how the world receives you, then you probably should quit when you feel you are not being successful and move on to something else.

On the other hand, if you have a strong desire for success and a personal passion for a project with a potentially big payoff, then stick to it. Make a sound plan, get the job done, and do not let anyone stop you. Persist until you succeed.

Question: What's more important for success: perspiration or inspiration? I think it's more important to have a positive attitude than to simply be a hard worker. Is there any research on this?

The conventional wisdom is that a positive mental attitude is the master key to success. Studies about optimism show that optimistic people live longer, get better grades, and are healthier.

The reality is that people confuse optimism as it is studied in science with a positive mental attitude.

Optimism means that you don't always believe it is your fault. Optimism means that the bad stuff doesn't have to last forever. Optimism means that problems in one part of life don't necessarily mean that everything has gone wrong or will. As scientists look at optimism and measure it, optimism is a useful outlook on life.

Attitude is important in all aspects of life. Attitudes are important in persuasion and influence. Attitudes matter. But if you were looking to measure the things that contribute to a successful life, a positive attitude might only be a small portion of those factors.

A positive attitude or a negative attitude is largely subjective and the impact of either of those attitudes on achievement will vary from person to person. A lot of people equate a good attitude with a big smile or a happy outlook on life. Others equate a good attitude with a visible face of determination. Others believe that a good attitude is really a focused attitude.

No matter what you think a positive attitude is, it often becomes an end in itself and that can lead to frustration and dissatisfaction. When this happens, it tends to cause the extinction of the goals for which the person was cultivating a positive mental attitude.

Reality? You can have a lot of different kinds of attitudes and achieve or fail. Success is much more closely tied to behavior than it is to intention.

In my mind, I can still see the guy sitting down and playing the piano, his fingers moving over the keys like a bird flapping her wings. He just flew. The music was complex and beautiful. You never would have thought this guy a pianist. And he was truly amazing.

"How the heck do you do that?"

"My Mom used to make me practice an hour every day after school."

"For how long?"

"From the time I was four until I graduated high school."

"You really wanted to do that?"

"Not at first, not for a long time. But then I did, yes. I started to love it in junior high."

Same with Lance Armstrong, Kristy Yamaguchi, Carl Lewis, Einstein, Edison, Curie, Bell, Mozart, The Beatles, Gates, Oprah, and Trump. Same with everyone who succeeds at anything. They lived and worked many, many days and years with no reward. The reward came later.

Success Actions That Work: Research shows that optimism is important for success (and health). In addition, a positive mental attitude can grease the wheels of achievement and help you get along with others who can help you along the way to success. You will be more successful when you are nice to others. Studies consistently show that people with pleasing personalities have an easier time reaching success. Not only are they more level-headed in taking care of business, but they also draw people to them who are eager and willing to help. Be polite and appreciative. Show true interest in others and keep a sense of humor.

But a positive attitude can't be an end in itself or you will not accomplish all that you are capable of. If we had to choose, we would pick perspiration over inspiration. But you need and can have both.

In most cases, behavior precedes attitude. Behavior (action) tends to generate passion for the behavior itself. If you want to be successful, *do* the things it takes to be successful. A positive or inspired attitude will follow shortly thereafter.

Question: **How important is focus and concentration to high achievement? Some days I can be really scatterbrained. Will this affect the level of success I**

achieve in life? Are there things I can do to improve my focus?

Focus and concentration are central to achieving at a high level. It takes concentrated effort to play the game of life with optimal results. For 2,000 years, great achievers have mastered the ability to concentrate. In art and science, business and warfare, literature, politics and philosophy, the real achievements of humankind have been the result of this power.

Concentration arises chiefly from being deeply interested or vested in an activity. It is very closely related to persistence and what Napoleon Hill called "definiteness of purpose." Concentration is the enemy of self-consciousness and vacillation. Timid people are erratic in their habits. They shift constantly from one thing to another, appearing to be busy but accomplishing nothing substantial. Concentration enables us to accomplish incredible things.

Concentration is the art of continuous and intense application to a task. To cultivate concentration you must have focus. At first, it's a good thing to think and do only one thing at a time. There's nothing wrong with writing a book and doing home improvements in the same 30-day period. There is everything wrong with starting projects and not finishing them. The creation of one bad habit after another destroys the most crystal clear dreams.

Developing concentration is a pillar of long-term success. It is fairly easy to tell if someone will succeed or not. The question: Do they get things done?

Do *you* get things done? Despite your "scatterbrained" moments, do you have the power of concentrated effort? If not, and you do not do something to change, you are destined to do the same thing everyday for the rest of your life.

Here is a secret that might improve your long-term focus: *No one can become deeply interested in work that they don't like.*

Thousands of people struggle upstream all their lives because they are in a job that doesn't fit them. They do not experience doing their best—and the fulfillment that flows from this—because they do not like what they are doing and lose their own self-respect. Are you one of them?

It is easiest to improve focus and change behavior in general when you integrate an emotional component. This means that you can reduce the need to white knuckle your way to high achievement through sheer determination and hard work. You can go beyond a logical connection to your effort and feel the emotion of why you are doing what you do.

Unfortunately, we can't give you the emotional component that will keep you focused. You have to find that. What is the one thing that drives you, the one thing that matters more than anything else? It has to be real and it has to engage you. Stopping can't be an option because the emotional component of missing the goal is more engaging than the temporary pleasure of not doing whatever is required to enhance your skill or competence. Your ability to dig in, to stay focused, to get up one more time, to practice when you don't want to, to reach further than your peers, and to put temporary pleasures aside will allow you to more quickly achieve your goals.

Success Actions That Work: In order to cultivate focus, you must bring your will to bear strongly upon your work and your life. Begin to develop your focus skills today in little things. Cultivate intense focus in whatever you do. Say to yourself: "This is one thing I do and I will do it well until it is done." Period. Develop your ability to focus and complete projects by reading guides in this area such as *The Power of an Hour* (Lakhani 2006). Perhaps you need a mentor who will help you see how most every difficulty yields to the power of focus and how uninterrupted application to one thing will achieve the seemingly impossible.

Without concentrated focus, you will be unable to persevere in the face of difficulty. By contrast, a person of strong will and concentration uses obstacles as stepping-stones to higher things. Don't be one of those people who complain that they don't like the idea that they lack focus, concentration, and memory, but then don't make the slightest effort to improve themselves. All the goals in the world are meaningless without focus, concentration, and effort.

One of the payoffs of increased concentration is an improved ability to make more money and better manage it. Yet, the need for concentrated effort goes beyond business. You want to increase your ability to concentrate in nonincome producing activities, too. Apply intense focus to everything you do. Why? Because the power of concentrated effort will help you cultivate many other valuable traits like organization, punctuality, thoroughness, an improved memory, self-respect, and self-reliance. Through concentrated effort you will not only aspire to but attain the highest achievements.

2

The Game Plan

High performers make and follow a game plan. Watch a football game. The coach carries a big two-sided laminated 11 × 17 sheet of paper with him during the entire game. He covers his mouth with it when he speaks into the microphone to tell the quarterback what play to call. There are hundreds of plays on that laminated sheet of paper.

They are all based upon the precise situation the team is in. Are they ahead in the game? Behind in the game? Is the game tied? Is it first or second down? Do they have the ball at their 20-yard line? Midfield? How about at the opponent's 20?

The coach has already analyzed his own team. He knows his players' strengths and weaknesses, their skills and deficiencies. He and his assistant coaches factor in the other team's strengths, weaknesses, and behavioral tendencies *in any given situation* as they prepare for the game.

They know that the other team passes 85 percent of the time when it is third down and 6 yards to go and 97 percent of the time when they are near midfield. Such knowledge makes defending against the other team a little easier.

They know what's coming. They have watched their behavior all year and know what they do in specific situations ... in every situation. They've gathered the intelligence and put it into a game plan.

Don't confuse a game plan with a business plan.

A business plan, the way most of us were taught to write one, is usually a big waste of paper and time. It gives you a best case scenario. It gives the bank the best-case scenario. It tells you nothing about what is really going to happen with the business, how all situations will be managed, and what plays will be called.

The business plan doesn't assume that your advertising will fail. (It will.)

It doesn't assume that your salespeople will have more turnover than anticipated. (They will.)

It doesn't take into account all the random weird stuff that happens every day in business, like getting sued by the guy who tripped on the sidewalk in front of your business because his grocery bag was too thin—you get the idea.

A business plan is far better labeled "a business hope."

Are we saying a business plan is a complete and utter waste of time? No. It does not take a lot of time to come up with a basic plan for a million dollar business. Is it valuable and meaningful? No. Is it necessary to get your loan? Probably.

A game plan for your business is based on an analysis of all of the variables *and has an action called for each specific situation*. It takes into account what happens when an employee steals or someone plants an untrue story about your company in the press.

The game plan requires thought. It requires understanding *situational management strategy*.

The business owner with a powerful game plan is going to achieve.

But wait! Sports teams use game plans. The Houston Texans only won two games last year. Their coach surely had a game plan and it didn't do them any good. What's going on there?

Nothing is going on there. The team is achieving to its level of ability and skill. It is a new team filled with new players who are learning to work with each other. Generally speaking, the team has a few guys with talent but the reality is that it doesn't have the skills and talent to compete. That they won even two games is a testament to their desire to win.

Achieving isn't always measured in wins and losses. It's measured in achievement relative to potential. If you have a high school team playing a professional team and the high school team somehow keeps the game close, they would achieve an enormous victory even in defeat.

The game plan can't completely make up for a lack of skill, talent, and self–discipline, but it sure can make the difference between winning and losing. It can give a weaker opponent a shot at beating a stronger opponent.

A business plan? Okay, fine. The bankers will feel better if you have one, so you make it for them.

For you? You need a game plan.

Question: I have heard both that I should set outrageous, bodacious goals and that I should set easy, baby step goals. Do these approaches conflict with each other? Or should I use different types of goals depending on what I'm trying to achieve?

In general, bodacious goals will produce a higher level of performance than smaller, safer goals. Research shows that two things will determine in large part how effective a goal is. Goals should be *difficult* and *specific*. Now, that doesn't mean that you will attain the goal. It means that these two factors support high performance and the best overall results.

When setting difficult goals, be sure you do the mental work to ensure that you see the goals as challenging but not too difficult. If you see a goal as impossible to achieve, your brain will tell you that there is no reason to work toward it and will shut down any efforts to try. Set goals that you must stretch to achieve, but be sure that they do not seem impossible or unachievable.

The more specific and challenging the goal, the more likely it is to encourage high performance. Let's say you want to earn $100,000 next year. That's a good goal. A better goal would be to earn $131,400. Your brain will perceive this as more specific (and a little more difficult) and you will likely put forth a better performance.

Notice that we are talking more about using goal setting as a method to improve performance rather than to achieve any particular goal. Usually, hitting a goal right on the nose is not very important in life. What is important is that striving for goals helps keep you on track. If you set $131,400 as an income goal, do you *really* care if you make $131,399 or $131,401? What is important is that you perform well.

You will know when you are in the ballpark. Setting a goal of $131,400 and earning $117,000 is an indication of high performance. Setting a goal of $150,000 and earning only $105,000 indicates that you need to tweak your goal achievement process. What matters is increasing and optimizing performance with specific and difficult goals that are possible and believable. And you must have some kind of feedback system to help you know that you are on track.

Success Actions That Work: There is nothing wrong with setting easy or baby step goals. Just realize that they lead to much poorer overall performance than do difficult goals. Try setting more difficult goals and see what happens. Break down the big goal into a series of realistic targets. Give yourself a timetable by which to reach each target and review your progress on a regular basis to make sure you are on track.

Question: How does goal setting work to improve performance, and what is the biggest reason people don't stick with goals?

Goals help alter performance in a variety of ways. Some of these include:

1. Goals direct attention and effort toward the right activities (assuming the person knows what he is doing).
2. They arouse effort to the level required by the task.
3. They promote the search for logical action plans or task strategies.
4. Goals encourage persistence.

When setting a goal, the least acceptable result you are willing to tolerate is a powerful measure of effectiveness and performance. Regardless of what's written on a piece of paper, often your least acceptable result is the goal that you will achieve.

The biggest antagonist to achieving goals can be summed up in the phrase "instant gratification." You want to achieve your goals? Focus on stopping the desire for instant gratification in its tracks.

For example, your goal is to lose 22 pounds. You see food that isn't on the agenda. Your brain wants instant gratification. In fact, it all but *demands* it. If you want to have any hope of achieving your goals, you need to put the food away, lock it up, and distract yourself from instant gratification.

When people are trying to lose weight, they should do things like take a walk everyday. Because a walk will help burn calories? That's part of it. But it's not nearly as important as being away from food for 30 minutes while their cravings fade. When you are out for a walk you are not near the refrigerator. And therein is a secret of success. Do something to get away from the possibility of instant gratification and you move closer toward your goal. If that distraction contributes to the achievement of the goal, so much the better.

What else can you do to increase your chance of successfully achieving your goals? There is a lot of science behind goal achievement and high performance. Research shows there are factors that affect goal achievement and make it more (or less) likely that a person will achieve a goal. Some of these include relevance, feedback, and self efficacy.

Relevance: Know what's behind your goal. This increases the relevance and intensity of the goal. In goal attainment, understanding the "why" is about as important as anything. If you have a compelling enough reason why you want to do something, you can accomplish darn near anything. You will be most committed to achieving a goal when you believe that achieving the goal is important.

Feedback: Incorporating a feedback loop that allows you to make corrections along the way will increase the likelihood of achieving a goal. When feedback shows progress toward the goal, you get the best results. For example, you want to earn $131,400. You see yourself at $81,000 in July and you know you are on your way based upon the simple math of the goal. An important form of feedback comes from other people such as coaches or accountability partners with whom you have shared your goals and who continue to monitor your progress toward achieving them.

Self efficacy: People are more likely to perform well when a goal is seen as attainable based upon their knowledge, their training, and their skills. Mastering a certain skill or expertise increases your confidence that you can achieve your goals in this area. Knowing that you have skill and can affect outcomes is called self efficacy. When people know things can happen because they can make them happen, performance increases.

Success Actions That Work: Here is the secret to becoming a top performer: Get really good at something. When people with a high degree of self efficacy set goals, they tend to choose more difficult goals, are more committed to the achievement of those goals, choose better task strategies, and respond with more energy to all kinds of feedback.

As self efficacy increases, goals become less necessary. People with high degrees of self efficacy will perform at a very high level without goals. Getting good at something and having confidence goes a long way toward achieving at a high level.

Our personal experience as high achievers is in line with the research. At an elite level of performance in an area in which you are accomplished, goal setting takes a backseat to a project focus. You take on projects, make commitments, and know what has to be done in the next three or six months. These things get done because you have become the type of person to make it happen. Or you make decisions along the way that something else more important will take the place of a certain project and you get that done instead.

With discipline and a lot of practice, you will find that goal setting, task concentration, persistence, and completion become almost hardwired. So you may find as you perform at a higher and higher level, you stop thinking in terms of goals and start thinking in terms of desires, targets, projects, outcomes, and journeys. It will become less necessary to use a formal goal setting system. Top performers know what has to happen and they simply get those things done.

Question: I am trying to break into informational marketing. It seems most of the support material I read emphasizes speed—getting products out quickly. Maybe I'm old school, but I am not willing to put something out with my name on it that is not of the highest quality.

I really believe the long-term payoffs will be there. What do you think is more important for success: speed or quality?

Both matter.

Quality matters. No matter what you do in life, doing it well *is* the great reward. Whether this applies to your work or your health, your relationships or your personal goals, making a commitment to personal excellence in whatever you do virtually guarantees the foundation to a life of fulfillment, success, and passion.

As with most things in life, the results we experience tend to be in proportion to the quality and intensity of effort we put forth. If we don't go for it, we experience minimal results. If we give our absolute best, we increase our chances of getting results (even if they aren't what we initially intended). Sometimes the results are better than we expected.

But speed and completing projects matter, too. You don't get paid if you don't finish things. Often, the first one out of the shoot wins the race. High achievers move quickly.

The answer to this balance between speed and quality lies in understanding the law of diminishing returns. This law states that quality increases in direct relation to time and effort in the initial phase of a task, but after a certain level of quality is reached, it takes much greater amounts of time and effort to affect changes in quality.

For example, you can cut your half-acre lawn in about 90 minutes and do an "A" job, getting 97 percent of the grass cut and missing just a little along the edges or under the steps of the deck. Or you can cut your half-acre lawn in 3 hours and do an "A+" job, getting 100 percent of the grass cut and missing nothing.

In most things in life, it makes sense to shoot for the A to A– range. There are a few things that require perfection, but usually the 97 percent is the way to go. Most things require being awesome but awesome is not perfection. You don't need the airline pilot to land perfectly, just perfectly safely. You do need him to land.

People who require perfection of themselves or others are very likely to *not* succeed in most of their ventures. Perfection becomes procrastination in many cases. It becomes an excuse for accomplishment. It becomes a factor in delay.

In almost all fields, perfectionists are mediocre performers.

Sound like a paradox?

It's not.

Do not confuse perfection with excellence.

Excellence means you give everything you have to give all day to the people who are your customers, your clients, your friends and others of your choosing. Are you awesome at what you do? Do you give your best effort? You must have some ego involvement or you will not be effective at what you do. You have to have a sense of pride in your work.

There is rarely a definition of perfection. There is no rulebook that tells you what perfect is. Does perfect mean you never make a mistake? That's not going to happen. Does perfect mean that everyone likes you? That's not going to happen.

Do we as professional speakers strive for excellence? Yes. We must be awesome. We have to be filled with energy so that we light up the bulbs in everyone's minds. We need to turn on everyone's thinking apparatus. We want to stimulate our audience for emotional impact and give them takeaways that they can use in real life. Being the best speaker is different from being the best writer, which is different from being the best entrepreneur and that is different from being the best information marketer.

Success Actions That Work: The pinnacle of performance is excellence, not perfectionism. There is no perfection in speaking, writing, creating, or in what you do on a daily basis. If there were, there would be no creativity, no desire, no excitement, no love, no happiness . . . just perfection.

Good for you to have high standards. Personal excellence is a prerequisite to success. Maintain high standards of quality, but do not do so at the expense of completing projects. Create a great product. Give it one more read through or run through to get you to that 97 percent. Then put it out there and move on to your next project.

Question: **There's a lot of buzz about "maps" or "mind maps" and "game plans." Are these really important and what is the best way to use them? My experience is that maps don't work.**

The question is really dealing with three different things and it is easy to see why it is confusing.

When people refer to maps they are often using an analogy to say "you'll get wherever you are going faster if you have a map to lead you there." The problem is that some people make it too complicated and substitute planning their route for action.

The likelihood of success is definitely enhanced if you create a simple "back of the napkin" plan that demonstrates your current status, the proposed outcome, and what you need to do to get there. This type of map keeps you on track and focused, and it allows you to quickly adjust and refocus when you are off track.

A game plan is much more of an implementation plan. In other words, when you engage, what do you intend to accomplish, how will you do it, and how will you address unexpected feedback while engaged? It is very common to hear athletes speak of following their game plan. They have an idea going into competition what they will do, how they will respond to their opponents, and how they will handle setbacks and challenges. A game plan is really more of a mental model than a map and it allows you to implement your specific strategies.

Game plans and strategies are essential to a high level of achievement. Success without a strategy isn't replicable success, it is luck. Once you make a decision about how you'll achieve success, you need to design a strategy that will work to keep you focused on your outcome. The strategy should include how you'll respond in times of uncertainty, stress, or unexpected results. How will you know when you need more information, when you need to apply a different tactic or strategy, and how will you know you've been successful? A good game plan begins with a clear definition of success.

Where maps and game plans are big picture strategies, mind maps are tactical. A mind map is a form of visual thinking derived from semantic networks of knowledge representation. Mind maps have been used for centuries in some forms but have been most recently popularized by British author Tony Buzan.

If you organize ideas visually, mind maps can be a great way to organize your thoughts or build an overall plan for success. They are, however, not mandatory for success, and there is no evidence that suggests there is any connection between success and mind maps.

Success Actions That Work: A broad map and a more specific game plan will help provide direction and clarity about how you are going to achieve your goals. Many high-level thinkers use mind maps in brainstorming sessions and find them useful for thinking through ideas. Mind mapping is also a very efficient note taking modality. You can learn about mind mapping with a quick Google search or by using the software developed by Mindjet.com. Also visit Bestsuccessfactors.com for more information on success rituals and plans.

At the end of the day, whatever method you use for organizing your plan for achieving success it is important that success is in the action and not in the planning. A simple plan with massive effort in execution, evaluation, and reengagement will always lead to greater success than a plan without initiation.

3

Directed Action

If you are not happy with what you have now, or who you are in life, then the only one who can make a difference to your situation or life is you. A change could mean altering your outlook on life, your outlook on yourself, your priorities, or your activities. You have no one else to blame but yourself and only you have the power to change your life.

For the vast majority of people, what goes around comes around. You only get back in life what you are willing to put into it. If you are helpful, honest, and a good person, then you will get the same back in return, which can help you on your path to success, particularly in the workplace.

Change, by definition, requires movement. And movement is not inertia. It is action.

But action by itself will not create success. *Directed action* is a necessity for success. Directed actions that are part of a plan with contingencies are the ultimate cause of successful change.

Change is uncomfortable. So, you need to get comfortable being uncomfortable. Choose to be uncomfortable. Know that being uncomfortable is probably a very good sign that you are on the road to making something good happen.

Directed action is about focusing on the outcome you want and the process of getting there. This does not mean you should focus only on the positive and what it is you want to achieve and ignore the negative or what it is that you don't want to achieve. Only unsuccessful people visualize good things, and only good things, and then move forward with foolish pride.

Directed action requires that you be a reality-based optimist. This comes from research conducted by Dr. Martin Seligman, the premier researcher who has quantified the power of non-negative thinking and written about it in his book *Learned Optimism*. Norman Vincent Peale wrote about the same phenomenon in his book *The Tough-Minded Optimist*.

Non-negative thinking is not positive thinking per se. It's not about some illusionary and invisible magical thinking. It *is* about evaluating results and refocusing for the future.

Reality-based optimism means you know bad things will happen. Period. When those bad things happen, you will get back up and work hard to pick up the pieces after the storm so you can keep moving toward your desired outcomes.

Reality-based optimism means you do not personalize defeat. Sure, it might be your responsibility that you lost XYZ. But that doesn't mean that *you* are the problem. You tripped. Big deal.

Reality-based optimism means you do not generalize defeat. Having lost at one thing today doesn't in any way mean you will lose in all aspects of life. You don't put eternal life into defeat. Today's defeat is today's defeat. Period.

Never let yourself entertain beliefs that today's failure is pervasive, permanent, or personal. It's not.

Reality-based optimism is about you being in control of your life, choosing to eliminate self-doubt, and creating your own luck.

You have charted all the fallen bridges and have detours and alternate routes planned. Ignoring the fallen bridge because it is a negative just means you will sit at the end of the road waiting for years for someone to build your manifestation for you. The successful person maps the journey after learning about the obstacles, fallen bridges, and flooded plains.

Have you ever heard someone say, "I'd rather be happy than successful?" The statement is all but meaningless except in one way. You know the person is neither happy nor successful; that individual is inert and not taking action toward becoming more successful.

Do not buy into this type of mentality. A belief that to be successful is to be unhappy or to be happy is to be unsuccessful is ludicrous. The two are not related (except, perhaps, when people's core needs for food, water, shelter, clothing, and safety are not being met).

Set a higher standard for yourself. Demand and create both happiness and success in your life. Starting today, take directed action toward accomplishing what you want to accomplish.

When coaching people who want to achieve something new we nearly always leave them with one action step that they have to take the minute we have finished. Why? Because we want them to have the experience of engaging immediately and getting a result. Most people already have had plenty of experience not engaging. This is a key factor in why they haven't reached most of their dreams and goals.

Setting a direction and taking action toward it comes down to *investing in yourself.* What is an investment? In a financial context, it is money we allocate (to a fund or program) with the intention to expand and grow it (with interest or other gains) so we get more money back.

How does this apply to our daily actions? If we see our every action as an investment, it means that we stand to gain more than we give.

If we invest in our personal growth and development, we gain a greater understanding of ourselves, our aspirations, and our potential.

If we invest in our complete health (mental, physical, emotional, and spiritual), we grow stronger and enable ourselves to continually produce powerful results.

If we invest in our careers by giving our best effort, continuing our education, and striving for long-term advancement, we gain more money, greater job satisfaction, and more opportunities for success.

If we invest in our relationships by strengthening communication and spending quality time with loved ones, our relationships grow and expand into meaningful connections that enrich our lives. It is exactly the same for everything you do, whether you are working on your passions or your obligations.

Would you want to have an operation done by a surgeon who was only half paying attention to what he or she was doing?

Would you want to be driven by a taxi driver who was only half watching the road?

Would you want to eat a meal that was only half cooked by a chef?

Why should the results you produce in your life be any less important? Invest in yourself. Invest in every move you make—completely, fully, wisely, and continuously.

Question: Taking action is left out of a lot of philosophies being read by salespeople. I want to teach my people that thinking is great but taking action is needed. How do you convince the team?

We see your problem. People who are responsible for getting others to get projects completed or sales calls made, their kids to get their homework done, themselves to get the grass cut are often unable to get past the well-intended thought.

To make matters worse, many managers have been taught that the answer lies in the "take action" mantra. Although this is certainly well intended, action is not in and of itself enough. "Get out there and see a lot of prospects," "open the books and study," and so forth are good first steps, but they don't really get to the core of success.

The reality is that taking *some* action is probably better than taking no action, but what happens in real life is that people move around a lot. They have meetings and sessions and all kinds of things that are really little more than busywork.

In general, an actor has more chances of succeeding than a person who relies on visualization to produce results, but the two are very close to each other in ultimate achievement. People who simply take action, often end up taking useless actions that lead to burnout and all kinds of other problems. You need to ask the right questions. Taking what action? When? How? With whom? Why?

In most facets of business and life in general, we want certain results. We want to have more money. We want to have a smaller waist. We want to have a family that experiences more moments of joy than it used to. Each of these examples has something in common. They are all measurable. When you can measure you can predictably succeed.

For example, you want more money. When you work backward from that result, you realize that there are many paths to that result. Without figuring out which paths you're going to work on and in, you will probably fail.

There are so many ways to make more money that doing so requires that you make conscious decisions. Some options:

- You can save your money.
- You can invest your money.
- You can work more hours.
- You can make more sales.

- You can make bigger sales.
- You can sell to the same person more often.
- You can have more places where people can buy your products and services.
- You can get a second job.

And on and on.

There are many options. There is no "default" for the brain so nothing happens even when you take action.

Conscious attention, conscious intention, and application become critical if one is to earn more money.

You must make decisions about what you are going to do to make more money. Upon analyzing all the variables, you figure out which options make most sense for your short- and long-term goals, and then you begin working on those projects every day.

Eventually those actions you take as you work on the individual projects will become new habits and you will default to these actions instead of playing video games. You will make more money because you will be carrying out the specific actions (projects) that will yield that result.

This distinction is one of the most important in the pursuit of achievement. If you want to achieve something or have your team achieve something, you must determine how you want that to happen. Determine which steps you will take. Then every day you work on those steps until they become habit or second nature.

When that happens your brain is reset for that result. Once there, it won't need to be reset again until you move into new territory for making more money.

Remember doing mazes as a kid? They became easier when you figured out a strategy: Start at the end and work your way to the beginning, or at least work backward to a point that is reachable from the start. This strategy still works.

In another example mentioned earlier, you want a waistline that is two inches smaller. You can work backward from that result and realize that some combination of less food, more activity, and time will accomplish that result.

You want your family to experience more moments of joy? That's an end result. It's measurable. You can identify what kinds of experiences cause your family to experience joy. By encouraging your family members to participate in those specific activities or experiences, you are likely to reach the desired outcome.

Success Actions That Work: Taking action is useful only as a starting point. It is like wanting to go to New York from wherever you are. You hear "take action" so you put the car in drive and go. You might end up in New York, but you wouldn't want to bet on that. Taking action is getting into drive. It is a darned important place to start and then move on from onto a specific path that has been planned and laid out.

We do not want to diminish the idea of starting. We simply want to make sure that you remember that taking action without direction accomplishes little more than standing and moving. It's better than sitting and being inert. It increases the chances of getting somewhere. But it will not put you on the fastest track to reaching your destination.

In order to fast-track your team to success, help each person determine where they want to go. Specify how they are going to reach their specific goals. What are they actually going to do to get there? Then build in accountability so that they do these things every day and move closer to achieving their goals.

Question: What's your opinion of The Law of Attraction from *The Secret*? Is there support for the notion that we attract everything into our lives and businesses?

The Law of Attraction as described by Rhonda Byrne in her book *The Secret* basically proposes that you attract everything you have into your life, good or bad. This happens through a universal resonance at the quantum or subatomic level where "like attracts like, the same as a magnet" (magnets do not attract like but rather the exact opposite, but we won't quibble over the minor points).

According to *The Secret*, if you win the lottery, you attracted it. If your child is a burn victim and dies, you attracted it. If your country is attacked, you attracted it. If a hurricane hits your city and destroys hundreds of thousands of lives, you all attracted it. If you are fat, you shouldn't look at other fat people if you want to lose weight. And, of course, it's just as easy to attract $1 as it is $10,000.

People who believe in the Secret tell us that the Law of Attraction is a scientific law, just like the law of gravity. This claim is jaw dropping. Who would believe it? Millions do.

No, there is no Law of Attraction that operates on the same level as the law of gravity. There are plenty of ways to show that it is not a scientific law. We could fill a book with all kinds of evidence that proves that the Law of Attraction as it is taught in the current "Secret" movement does not produce the promised results. But why don't you do a quick experiment yourself?

This scenario comes from *The Secret*.

Ask for $100,000.

Imagine the money arriving by courier tomorrow.

Get a clear picture of it in your mind.

Feel good about it.

Be grateful for it.

It will be there.

Take these specific steps as taught by *The Secret*. See for yourself if that check arrives.

We have seen a lot of damage done to innocent people who bought into the Law of Attraction as portrayed in *The Secret*. As we were writing this book, one author received an e-mail asking if the Law of Attraction could cure clinical depression. How scary. And sad. *The Secret* is misleading millions of people into a false sense of security, financial disaster, possible physical danger, lost homes, and broken families. The guilt follows when people can't get this law to work for them.

Here is how you can really use your brain to get more of what you want in business and life. The human brain is an amazing creation. It helps you filter through endless stimuli based on what it has been taught is important or not important. You get to attend to a very small percentage of what is really out there. The brain directs you to pay attention to what it knows is important.

As you think about things or have thoughts triggered by seeing or hearing something, your brain will look around the environment to find stuff that is related to those triggers. For example, you hear a phone ring. You look in the direction of the ring. You get up to see there is no phone. It is upstairs. You go look for it and find it. You do all of these things without much thought because you were triggered to do so.

To say it in a rudimentary fashion, the brain is a trigger-seeking device. Whenever the brain is triggered with something that is novel or has previously been related to something important in some way to it, the brain focuses attention on things that are related to the trigger.

If you are a librarian at school and you are typing away at your computer during the news, you will not remember much of anything about the news. But if your auditory system picks up that a school had a bomb threat or that some library was awarded a huge grant to buy books, you'll look up and watch even if it isn't your school. The brain is continually scanning "out there" for stuff that is important to it.

Your brain does not attract information. It cannot bring information to you from somewhere else. You will have to go get it yourself. But, it can be trained to make you aware of things that you normally would not have been aware of through prior programming.

Success Actions That Work: Decide what you want to see happening in your life. Think about who you want to meet, what you want to be doing with your life, what type of wealth you want to create, and what type of contribution you want to make to the world. Create some good mental imagery of these things. Include the sounds and words others would say who are around you in these images. Make them clear and vivid. Do this for a few minutes until an emotion is generated.

Once you feel emotion, you have created one tiny trigger for the brain to pick up on when it encounters things related to these images in the real world. It won't always grab them for you, but you will increase the chances of your brain recognizing opportunities that you would not have seen before.

This is not a law. It is an effective strategy that works fairly consistently. It is a scientific fact that you can prime the brain to attend to certain future stimuli. It will not catch everything. It can't. The brain doesn't have enough conscious space in which to process everything it encounters. But it sure can catch some of the stuff out there that you have been missing and you will literally take a step in programming yourself for success.

Question: **I am learning a lot in my job and making connections to lay the groundwork for starting my own company in a couple years. It's a good springboard for**

me and I try to get the most out of each workday. Unfortunately, most of my coworkers seem to just be putting in time and they can be a big distraction. What time management strategies can I use to keep others from wasting my valuable time?

You have a lot going for you. One of the key ingredients for successfully managing your time is identifying your goals. Goals will keep you motivated and focused—two essential parts of being productive.

Goals and time management are inherently intertwined. When you have determined where you want your life to be in one year or farther down the road, it will have an impact on what you do today. A person who dreams of being a lawyer will not have much success obtaining that goal if he doesn't first make the time to fit studying and school into his schedule today.

Many long-term goals will have short-term goals that lead to them. Not only does this make practical sense (getting accepted to a law school is a shorter term goal than becoming a partner in a law firm) but it also helps keep you from becoming overwhelmed or losing sight of your goals.

You obviously understand the concept that there is a limited supply of time and it is all valuable. High achievers understand that while responsibilities at work and home may largely dictate how they plan their day, most of this time can work in harmony with their goals. For some, this may require some big changes. For you, it sounds like it may just mean adjusting some things in your daily routine.

When you start planning your time with a goal in mind it is easier to appreciate the benefits of what you are doing and prevents you from getting caught up in time wasting activities. These activities use up your time but are ultimately unprofitable both financially and in your personal life.

You are on the road to success. How do we know? It's fairly simple. People who are productive are worth more. People who are unproductive are worth less. It sounds like your organization is full of unproductive types.

We encourage you to make your focus less about time management and more about *time production*. Successful people understand the importance of efficiency and working smarter to sustain a high level of energy.

Let's look at some key ways in which people destroy productivity and profit in business. You cannot manage your time until you have some time to manage. So start by getting rid of wasted time. You also will need to draw boundaries to keep other people from wasting your time. Here are five big time wasters for you to think about and avoid.

1. Meetings

People who spend all day in meetings are not getting things done.

Meetings have their place (an annual meeting is a good idea!) Meetings can be an important way to deal with group issues, create plans and get feedback. Yet, few people understand how to make a successful meeting happen.

A common problem is managers who want to make their time seem important so they call their employees together for a meeting, but they have no plan or desired outcome. If the purpose of a meeting is unclear and participants are unprepared or simply come with their own separate agendas, the group will not make clear and quick decisions.

We challenge you to think about how necessary and productive the meetings are that you choose to attend. As we were writing this book, one of the authors received the following e-mail message: "The agenda for tomorrow's meeting is attached. At this point there is not much on the agenda." It probably goes without saying that she did not attend the meeting.

Do all that you can to avoid wasting time at meetings by asking that the person who organizes the meeting do the following:

- Create an agenda giving each item a time allotment. Prioritize the agenda so the most important issues are dealt with first and quickly.
- Send the agenda to all participants so they can come prepared.
- Avoid last-minute meetings. Plan the meeting a minimum of one week ahead of time.
- Focus on finding a solution—scheduling another meeting should not be the solution although it may be a part of completing the plan.
- Schedule meetings for the end of the day so that everyone involved can arrange their work flow and jump right into their tasks the next morning.

If there is nothing to discuss or an issue can be dealt with on the phone or through e-mail, do not hold a meeting.

2. Phone Calls

You do not have to answer the telephone every time it rings.

Think of this: If your children are safe and sound and yet you go to the phone every time it rings, you have reduced yourself to the level of Pavlov's dog.

Bell: Salivate.

Ring: Pick up phone.

Don't do it!

If you have blocked out a certain time for working on a task, do not let phone calls interrupt your momentum. While you may feel that you always need to be "on call," the truth is that you are losing productivity by permitting continual interruptions to your work flow.

Successful people rarely answer the phone. Exceptions? Sure there are. But think of what happens when you answer the phone. You talk and talk and talk. Or the caller does. You waste more time getting back to . . . let's see . . . where did you leave off?

Unless you get *paid* to answer the phone, let it ring. If you must answer the call and the person can wait, ask them for a time when you can call back and discuss the issue. Not only will you set boundaries with your time, it will help you prepare to deal with the call without other distractions.

To avoid wasting time with phone calls try the following:

- Turn off your phone while you complete your task. If this is too much for you at first, start with one or two hours.
- Ask that your calls be held for the allotted time (making exceptions for those who must have access to you, like your boss).
- If you answer, tell the caller that you are in the middle of a task and only have a few minutes to resolve the issue. If this can't be done, schedule a return call later that day. Decide who will make the return call and when.

Remember, phone calls at home also eat up your time. This is time that you could be spending with family or on activities of your choosing. To break your phone answering habit, try this. Start a house rule that whoever picks up the phone has to talk to the person even if they are calling to talk to someone else. Have them take a message. It really can be this simple.

3. Drop-in Visitors

"Do you have a minute?" never really means do you have one minute? It will always take longer.

Banish drop-in visitors and replace them with three categories of visitors. There are people who have an open invitation and you tell them that. There are people who see you by appointment. There are people who don't see you. Period.

If you cannot finish a task without a coworker stopping in to ask for a minute of your time, you likely will lose whole days as that individual becomes preoccupied with one-minute issues. Often the person will get comfortable and want to discuss many more items than the one that initially spurred the interruption. Let your colleague hire a therapist. You accomplish your work so you can have time to get your projects done and be with the people you want to be with.

While some positions do require an open-door policy or you may not have an office you can close the door to, it is important to have uninterrupted time in your day to complete the tasks on your list.

To avoid wasting time with drop-ins try the following:

- Close the door or use a do-not-disturb sign to discourage idle visitors.
- If you must deal with a situation or individual, ask for a brief description of the details and then suggest you find a time to sit down and discuss it. Schedule a meeting so your colleague knows you view the issue as important and want to set time aside to discuss it.
- Remind yourself that saying no to others allows you to say yes to your own priorities.

4. Working at the Wrong Time

Do you plan activities that clash with other people's schedules? Do you find that the time you allotted to make calls (such as lunchtime) means you are not able to get a hold of anyone? Do you seem to ask for help when everyone else is too busy?

Do not waste your resources. Rearranging your schedule to make the most of your time will prevent you from getting in your own way. Proactively reviewing your schedule and finding the most opportune times for tasks will make your day much more productive.

To avoid wasting time with bad scheduling try the following:

- Do you find others want to stop by and talk with you toward the end of the workday? Use this time to make all of your return calls. If coworkers want to talk to you at this time, tell them it will have to wait until after work. This will help them get right to the point.
- Do you often need to ask for assistance with big projects? Plan ahead so that your project does not conflict with other people's schedules.
- Give yourself extra lead time. Things don't always work out like you plan. Give yourself some extra time so you can make your deadlines even if you have setbacks. Check up on delegated tasks to make sure they're on schedule and give them early deadlines as well.
- Become aware of your energy cycles and schedule activities accordingly. If you are most alert first thing in the morning, block off this time with no phone calls or visitors so you can throw yourself into your projects.

5. Disorganized Work Space

To use your time well, you must have an organized work space. Every moment you spend looking for a pen, a document, or a misplaced file not only means wasted time but it can add to your stress level and interfere with your ability to focus on your work.

To avoid wasting time with a disorganized work space, try the following:

- Give *everything* a home. This applies to your home as well as your desk and includes your mail, cell phone, and keys.

- Keep items you need daily easily accessible. Whether you work from your car or an office, place phone lists, calendars, and other frequently consulted items in an easy to see spot or in an easily accessible folder. Put everything else away.
- Put away files and tools that are not in use. The easiest way to do this is to give yourself at least 50 percent more storage space than you currently need. If you cram items into a small space, you will not likely keep up with your organizing and you will have difficulty finding what you need.

Success Actions That Work: Did you see yourself in any of the five time wasters discussed above? Did this list trigger thoughts about other huge wastes of time in your life and at work? Once you have identified and dealt with key time wasters, you will be surprised how much more productive your day can be.

Use these time management tips as part of your bigger recipe for success. Define what you want to achieve and connect your use of time to your goals. Make smart decisions (sufficient sleep, healthy food, exercise, and regular breaks) to produce more energy and get more done. Get rid of time wasters and become even more efficient so you use your time to produce greater results more quickly. All of these things will serve you well when you make the jump to running your own company!

Question: I have a bad habit of putting stuff off until the last minute. I usually end up meeting deadlines but end up causing myself a lot of stress. How can I break this pattern?

Everyone has procrastinated at some point. We hear from a lot of people about this issue so do not think that this is something that only you go through. But you need to take care of it as quickly as possible so that you can take back the time you are losing. Conquering procrastination is unbelievably important to achieving at a high level in life.

Procrastination is putting something off for another day even though you have the ability and the time to complete that task right now. Usually people do this when they want to do something else that is a bit more fun or even just easier. Instant gratification.

Research shows that procrastination is least likely when you expect to successfully complete the project, value completing the task, have a tight deadline, and don't have a personal dislike for the task. It largely comes down to the desirability of the task. The more you view the task as appealing, the more likely you are to tackle it and get it done.

Waiting until the last minute to get your work done causes a variety of problems that can wreck your day and your schedule. When you procrastinate, you often fall short of producing your best work, and that can cause you to miss out on opportunities for success in many ways. Procrastination can ruin your career because it may show others that you are unable to achieve your goals. You probably procrastinate in varying amounts everyday and are not even aware of all of the disruptions.

So, how can you get moving again? Start by learning to identify what is happening and knowing how to react when you begin to procrastinate. When you realize that you are procrastinating or are about to, you can stop it and get back on track to better manage your time. That's the behavioral strategy and it's a good one.

It is important to keep a list of your tasks. This way, you can weigh everything out on paper and prioritize tasks. People who don't use a list to manage their time are like shoppers who shop without a list. Go to the store with a list, you buy what's on the list, and you're out in 30 minutes. Go to the store without a list, you spend 50 percent more money, and it takes you 15 minutes longer. It works the same way in business and in life. Have a list? You get stuff done. If you don't have a list, you are not going to be as productive.

A common problem in putting off the completion of tasks is that many people cannot prioritize their tasks. For example, you have an important task to complete. You also have an urgent task to complete. Which do you handle first? You should accomplish the important task because it is just that, important!

Far too many people look to accomplish the things that they think are necessary to complete right now, forgo the important task, and then need to find a way or a time to rebalance things in their favor. Imagine that you are working at your desk and in walks your boss. She needs you to handle an important client. The phone rings, and it is a coworker who is struggling to accomplish his task and wants your help. You get back to work. Your coworker calls again. He really needs you. Which task do you tackle? Do you take care of the important client or the coworker who will keep calling until you help him?

The task that you should be completing first is the one that is important, the one that needs your full attention and that will get you the most bang for the buck. Take care of the client and please your boss. Unfortunately, far too many people strive to accomplish the "urgent" task because that person has called, complained, gotten into their head, and is the loudest voice telling them what to do.

Stop.

Tell your coworker "No!" and get back to work on *your job.* Better yet, don't even answer the phone when you are working on your important project. Choices.

Success Actions That Work: When you react to another person who is trying to make his urgencies your priorities, you change the way that the day is flowing. If you accept this type of interruption, you will be stressed and overwhelmed as you go about your task of dealing with the important client. You'll also have to explain to the boss why you made the client wait, why the task was not completed soon enough, and in the end why the job was not done correctly (because you could not concentrate under the stress of a compressed deadline).

To break your procrastination habit, you need to take the right steps to better manage your time. Couple this with the mindset of being a person who handles priorities and gets things done. Top achievers understand that procrastination is a mindset that they cannot afford with the limited amount of time that they actually have to achieve what they want in life.

4

Decision Making

Everything you do in attempting to achieve and succeed is a waste of time *until* you decide.

Decision is the starting point of self-discipline. Decision is the starting point of success. Decision making is a source of enormous power.

Making good decisions quickly is a pillar of achievement.

The decision has to be made now. And then you don't make it again.

Learning to make rapid, effective decisions that you trust and rely on is a crucial, but often completely overlooked, factor in success and achievement.

Most people aren't where they want to be in life. You certainly may be, but you probably aren't, and that is okay. Either way, ultimately you are responsible for where you are. The decisions you made are your decisions.

Now, sometimes bad stuff happens that you aren't responsible for and it gets in your way and you feel like it locks you into a prison. You may feel trapped. You ended up that way because of the things that happened and because of the decisions you made along the way.

Here is a crucial and irritating fact: In most cases the bad stuff that happens in life is only as powerful as the lack of preparation that was made. Most bad stuff can be prevented or minimized with some foresight and preparation.

This is where people lack the ability to analyze their road to "now" and, without accurate analysis, they will believe that only the decisions they make from today forward will impact their future.

Not true.

The decisions you've made for years bring you to today and many of them you are stuck with for life. Other decisions will take time to get over.

Have you heard the term "house poor" . . . or even "car poor"? We see it every day. Take out a $40,000 loan to buy an SUV. In five years it will be worth $20,000 and you will literally work to pay for that SUV to get back and forth to work! If you are living to pay for transportation (or your house) and saving only a couple hundred dollars a month for retirement, you need to work on your decision making.

Whatever you are spending each month on transportation, you should be spending at least 50 percent more than that on your business or investments (or both). That's a decision you make *today*. Then, when the bad stuff happens, you have the money that you put into investments if you can't work. You have security and financial freedom.

Reality Point: You are responsible for you.

In order to succeed, you need to get real with yourself. You may feel you're in a helpless situation. You feel that way because of the decisions you have made. You will continue to feel that way if you decide to stay where you are. Nothing will happen that will change anything (except for the worse). You've got to make a lot of decisions if you are going to move forward and not let your life situations decay.

What does the habit of good decision making look like? Look at our ancestors who took great risks to escape to a better life and made a lot of decisions along the way.

They decided they wanted a better life.

They decided to get on a boat to escape their lives of desolation.

They built the boat.

They got on the boat.

They got a map.

They set sail.

They were willing to risk getting lost or dying.

They decided to begin again.

They arrived to a whole new set of problems.

They prepared to get sent back to start over.

They kept at it.

They repeated as necessary until they found their dream.

That's a lot of decisions and a lot of effort.

Much of the success in America comes from making decisions and putting out effort. Nothing compares to the journeys some immigrants undertake to actually get here. Many American kids, with their PlayStations, big-screen TVs and toys galore, are at a big disadvantage for achievement and success compared with immigrants who make life or death decisions and then actually follow through on them.

The good news is that you can make decisions to get out of whatever situation you are in and experience new life. You'll experience feelings that will at first be very uncomfortable and often cause fear. Eventually those feelings will inspire and empower you. They will enable you to further your journey of success.

No more looking around observing how certain others seem to be living that life of success that you are after.

It's decision time.

Making good decisions will propel you to success faster than making poor decisions. The only way to get better at making good decisions is to make more decisions. Then learn from the decisions that you make.

Don't be paralyzed by the grip of indecision. When faced with too many choices—pick one. Often you will not know what type of choice you have just made until many variables have played out. Of course, it is this very idea that can lead to that paralyzing grip.

Theodore Roosevelt said, "In any moment of decision the best thing you can do is the right thing, the next best thing is the wrong thing, and the worst thing you can do is nothing." This quote encapsulates the truth about decision making.

The right thing. Some decisions seem to come in a flash of original and almost divine inspiration. These are the decisions that are so good that you may wonder where they came from. Well, the answer is that they came from your persistence, preparation, and practice.

The wrong thing. You may at first regret such poor decisions; that's okay. The trick is to make that regret no more than a mere glance when compared to the long vision of the lesson to be learned from them. If a decision is so bad you just cannot learn from it, pat yourself on the back because at least you did something.

Nothing. This is an excuse that will surely lead to failure. You will never know if you would have made the right decision, and you lose the opportunity to learn from a poor decision. The only antidote to this is to do something.

What will you do the next time you are faced with a difficult decision? The choice is yours. Success awaits and it's just a few shifts in direction from failure. You decide.

Question: I have always had a tough time making decisions. I put a lot of energy into making a decision and then I continue to second-guess myself. This can be agonizing and exhausting. Do you have any advice to help me make good decisions and feel better about them?

For most people, making decisions is uncomfortable. Many people tend to procrastinate when it comes to making decisions. But successful people view decision making as a requirement of performing at their highest level. The more decisions you make, the more change will happen, and the more success you experience (and the more failure, of course.)

Making decisions in life-changing situations can be hard for everyone. After all, the choice you make will affect your life and those in your life. The route you choose might not be easily reversible or it might be impossible to change.

Obviously, knowledge and understanding are paramount. Developing a logical mindset will help. You need to collect enough information to be confident that you can make a good decision.

Quick and confident decision making is essential to achieving at a high level. If we stop and look back on some of the moments in our life that went wrong, we find that some of our biggest regrets result from faulty decision making.

There are many reasons why we make the wrong decisions in life and almost everyone will have made the wrong decision at some time in their life. Perhaps we went with our gut instinct when making a decision or we let ourselves be swayed by others.

Success Actions That Work: Following are 20 tips to help you with decision making:

1. Decisions are merely making a choice among alternatives. There are good decisions and bad decisions. How something ultimately turns out is not the issue. A good decision is what happens now, not how it turns out.

2. A decision based on feelings, instinct in unfamiliar territory, or lack of information about all the alternatives is a poor decision. Base your decision on probability of outcome and the value of outcomes.

3. Unless you are an expert in the field in which you are making a decision, never base your decision on what *feels* right.

4. If you're outstanding in a field, make your decisions quickly. If you're not, make sure you collect all of the facts that you need to make a good decision.

5. Review all the facts thoroughly before you make a decision. Once you have reviewed them, allow yourself time to think about them before drawing a conclusion and determining your decision.

6. Jot down notes when making a decision, write down all solutions and include all relevant information. By seeing it written down in black and white, sometimes the right answer becomes more obvious.

7. Write down all the pros and cons of the decision you make. This can help clarify your decision or help you to see any problems the decision might create.

8. Determine and write down the relative importance of various results. For example, is it more important to have a larger salary or to have a more flexible schedule?

9. Do not procrastinate. If you have a decision to make, set a timeline and make it.

10. Make one decision at a time. Never allow decisions to build up and force yourself to make them all at once.

11. If others will be affected by your decision, then get their input on the situation. This doesn't mean you have to do what they suggest, but you still need to let people be heard.

12. Look at the objective of the decision, the alternatives to the decision, and the risks of any alternatives to the decision.

13. When considering a decision, ask yourself what will go wrong as you follow through with each choice.

14. Fully brainstorm potential consequences of each choice. What could happen? What else? How will you handle those problems?

15. Visualize your decision in your head and follow it through in your mind while you imagine a large group of people you know watching you. This will help you better visualize all outcomes of the decision before actually following through on it.

16. Talk over big decisions with a trusted advisor. You might find it helpful to have someone debate you on important decisions. As you try to defend your initial position, you may see some weaknesses. Remember that being right or wrong is not important when debating. Focus on making the best decision.

17. Put faith in your ability to make a successful decision and your ability to follow it through.

18. Integrity matters. When you know the right thing to do according to your value system, make a decision to do it.

19. When you make your decision, let go of all the what-ifs. Do not allow yourself to give any more thought or energy to a decision once it's made. You've already foreseen the pitfalls and you know how you will respond when they happen. Move on.

20. Make a decision *and act on it*. Once you have committed yourself to your decision, go with it full out. Recognize that you cannot know with 100 percent certainty that it is the right one but once made, stick with it. Act.

Decisions. You don't have to like or not like them. You simply have to become good at making them. Gather the optimal amount of information, decide, take action, and don't look back.

Question: Is there anything to the saying that top 20 percent produces 80 percent of the revenue?

You are referring to the Pareto Principle, also known as the 80/20 Rule.

This principle is an extremely helpful concept for making decisions and managing your time and life. Its creator, the Italian economist Vilfredo Pareto, first wrote about it in the late 1800s when he noticed that people seemed to divide naturally into what he called the "vital few" (the top 20 percent in terms of money and influence) and the "trivial many" (the bottom 80 percent). Pareto eventually observed that nearly all economic activity was subject to this principle. It has continued to be extended and to stand the test of time.

The equation might not always be exactly 80/20, but there are several areas of performance and life in which this principle applies. For example, in the United States, the bottom 80 percent of households pay just 13.7 percent of income taxes. And the top 1 percent are now paying a record level of taxes. Last year, this group paid nearly 40 percent of income taxes. Sounds insane but it is true.

In business and other areas of life, you will see a disproportionate amount of results come from a tiny number of people. There are a lot of "free riders" out there and top performers pay for their ride. That is not going to change.

In every business, the very best salespeople outsell all the others by a wide margin. Many people (80 percent?) are not good at what they do. Being in the top 20 percent requires many choices along the lines of the success factors discussed in this book. Choices create excellence. Choices create time.

It is important for you to analyze and understand the situation that you are in. How well are you managing your time? The Pareto Principle says that in most situations, your unfocused energy is only providing you with a mere 20 percent of the results that you have. That means that the other 80 percent of results are derived from a mere 20 percent of your effort.

Really think about what this could mean in your life. This principle says that 20 percent of your activities will account for 80 percent of the value you produce, 20 percent of your customers will account for 80 percent of your sales, and 20 percent of your products or services will account for 80 percent of your profits. Perhaps for you it is not exactly an 80/20 ratio, but it is likely that you are putting a lot of work into achieving very little with that time.

Success Actions That Work: How can you use the Pareto Principle to your advantage? In short, you need to direct your attention to the parts of your day or your tasks that can deliver the most return for effort, rather than worrying about all of the smaller things in the meantime and accomplishing very little. Your goal is to get as much as you can from your time, as much bang for your buck as possible, without sacrificing too much time to accomplish any one task. By increasing your focus, you can reduce the amount of time necessary to complete each task.

Even if the key activities are much more difficult than the other ones, you must be disciplined and refuse to spend your time on any activities in the bottom 80 percent before you complete the top 20 percent projects. This requires a shift in mindset from being busy to being productive. Your ability to choose between a result-producing activity and a less important activity will help you become a higher achiever. This principle is all about making smart decisions and being disciplined enough to follow through.

When you learn to prioritize and manage your time appropriately so that you focus on your top 20 percent income generators, you will accomplish much more. You will find yourself in a better position in your business and in your personal life and free up extra time to be even more productive. This will put you in a position to achieve even greater accomplishments. No more treading water or just keeping up.

It will take some understanding and restructuring, but using the Pareto Principle to your advantage is likely to deliver big rewards.

Question: **Is there a connection between risk taking and success?**

Yes, there is a significant connection between taking risks and success. There also is a connection between these two things and the success habit of saying "yes" to opportunities as a way of deepening your experience. Often the opportunities you'll be presented with will seem risky but the reward will be high. Many people will choose not to take the risk, preferring the relative comfort of the predictable.

Rarely are the biggest dreams achieved without taking chances. Yet, people who are willing to take big risks also risk monumental failure. The willingness to move forward and take the chance, to leverage instinct and experience (developed from saying yes) will quite often lead you to breakthroughs and successes beyond most others' wildest dreams.

Develop your risk taking behavior and you'll achieve more faster than ever before. Fail forward. When you experience a setback or a failure, see it as an opportunity to develop a new way. One failure doesn't mean to give up on your hopes and dreams. Jean Paul Getty, the famous oil man, was searching for oil in the Arabian Desert and had spent all but a million dollars of his fortune in the early 1950s. His friends all encouraged him to take his last million dollars and go home but he was positive he was right.

And, it turns out he was. Four years after tapping into the Middle East Neutral Zone oil reserves, Getty became the richest man in the world.

Are we suggesting that you risk your fortune like Getty? This isn't necessary, although it might be a legitimate choice. It depends on how sure you are about what you are doing. One thing is for sure. The thing that you stop short of will never be fully realized by you. You've got to ask yourself how important your dream or goal is and what you are willing to risk to achieve it. If the costs come down solely to money, this is a renewable asset. You can always get more. You can go back to work, you can build a different business, or you can raise more capital. But once you give up on a dream and someone else realizes it and capitalizes on it, you can never get it back.

Of course, we're not advising that you jump off the Empire State Building. Looking before you leap is prudent. Be certain there are no trains coming from either direction, then drive across the tracks. It's that fundamental. While you hang back and wait for that moment when you'll feel ready to take the risk, opportunities are passing you by and your confidence actually decreases as you get locked into a state of inertia.

Success Actions That Work: In what area have you failed to take risks even though you really wanted to move forward? Do you see where you have held back in the past?

Once you identify the risks you want to take, there are two logical ways to proceed.

One way is to start small. If you're really terrified about taking a giant leap, take a small step instead. When you realize that you're still standing and nothing horrible has happened, you'll feel more comfortable and inspired to take another small step. Keep doing that, and before long the proverbial giant leap won't seem so frightening.

Alternatively, push yourself to take the giant leap anyway. This choice would not be for the faint of heart, but for the person who knows his fear is unfounded and is willing to face it head on. In other words, this works best for the terrified person!

High achievers overcome and vanquish fear by walking through it. Today ... and over and over again. The fear will dissipate. Trust us.

Learn to take on challenges in your everyday life and get comfortable with risk taking. Are you afraid of heights? Climb a mountain. Do you fear public speaking? Join Toastmasters or take a professional speaking course. Are you afraid of meeting someone who could become a new boyfriend or girlfriend? Strike up a conversation with all the interesting people you encounter every chance you get.

A life of fear is a life of limitations. A life of taking risks and walking through fear is a life of endless opportunity. You can decide to be a person of fear or you can decide not to be.

Question: I am not as successful as I thought I would be at my age. How do I know if I'm sabotaging my success? Are there certain things I should be looking for as clues?

Resistance to success can be seen through behaviors such as procrastination and negative thinking. Resistance can cripple any potential successes or be a blockade to keep successful living from flourishing.

How do you know if you're resisting successful living? It's not rocket science.

Are you in the same place now you were in three months ago? Six months ago? One year ago? If you are not moving forward, you are resisting successful living.

If you have not been moving forward, what you have been doing is like balancing on a fence. Momentum wants to pull you in one direction, while your exhaustion, fears or doubts are pulling you in another direction. It takes tremendous endurance to stay balanced between two powerful forces like that!

Since you are already working hard at staying stationary, it is a mathematically simple matter to shift your focus and redirect your energies to begin moving forward. But emotionally? It is not as easy as it sounds, is it?

It seems like a major leap to move from where you are to where you would rather be. Like here is you and there is the moon. Yet, there is probably just one significant thing that stands between you and your ability to move forward. This one thing will be different for everyone.

Review the following common reasons for getting stalled and see which is happening in your life.

Comfort

Why would anyone want to resist successful living? Because we are not hardwired for change. We get too comfortable to change. We all love familiarity and comfort. It feels good. It's cozy.

To succeed, you must depart from your comfort zone. If you do not push the limits and do some really different things, you decay. You have entropy. You have failure.

Think about what you do while in your comfort zone. You sit back and find pleasure in being mentally lazy or living in a way that is familiar. You begin to expect things to just happen. People often think they are supposed to lay back in a recliner and the world will wait on them.

This mentality will kill an achieving spirit . . . and the security of those that depend on the guy in the recliner. The comfort mindset is the enemy of achievement and security.

There is no such thing as an overnight success. Success does not come knocking at your door. Not when you are awake at least. In caveman terms, the successful lifestyle calls for you to go out and kill something and drag it home. If you want it, go get it. No animal ever came up to the Neanderthal's villa and said, "Hey bud, time to kill me so you have food for next week. Get off your butt and grab your spear . . . geesh." It just does not happen.

Taking action on something new is flat out uncomfortable. Face it. And then make a choice to not get too comfortable. Comfort is an enemy of achievement and success in everything from careers to relationships. Get out of your comfort zone and make things happen!

Habit

Habit can be an enemy of success or it can be the backbone for achieving success.

What are some habits that crush any chance of achieving success? You probably can write your own list. Some that stand out to us are a lack of self-discipline, laziness, complacency, and procrastination. Do any of these sound familiar? If you are not where you want to be, perhaps a couple of these bad habits need to be banished from your life.

One of the most difficult things to do is to stop a bad habit. And then, of course, another extremely difficult thing to do is to start a good habit. Now combine those and try to stop a bad habit and start a good habit at the same time. Two decisions and a lot of effort will be required.

Here's a good way to begin replacing bad habits with good ones: Get angry enough at your current circumstance that you D-E-C-I-D-E to make a change. The most effective tool for change is a concrete, rock solid, put-your-life-on-the-line-and-kick-your-butt decision.

Yes, it is much easier to think, "I deserve something good. Something fun." And that is true. We are not telling you to avoid the activities you enjoy. You need those things. You need to have a fun social life and plenty of downtime to relax and recharge. You need to take breaks throughout each day.

But you also need more than fun and relaxation. You need a sense of pride and accomplishment about what you do. If you are not doing meaningful work and not enjoying the level of success that you want and know you can achieve, it is time to take a close look at the bad habits that are holding you back.

High achievers share many common characteristics. And one of these is the habit of making good decisions and carrying through on them. Adopt this habit and it will bring more success in your life.

Fear

Fear can be the most crippling, unrelenting, paralyzing, scary emotion you will ever experience, if you let it be. Fear plays a part in our everyday lives. It can be a good thing and keep you safe from falling.

But it will keep you from taking risks. It will push you back toward that which is familiar. Consequently, it will keep you from successful living.

There is always a very reasonable question of the unknown element of success. You get it into your head that something bad will happen if you begin working toward what you want. You have a feeling of dread or doom. How will your life change if you really succeed? Or perhaps you focus more on the fear of failing.

What if you work hard at making something good happen in life, but you somehow mess it up and fail? It just feels easier to not try at all.

What should you fear more: taking a chance and possibly failing or never trying at all and creating a life of certain mediocrity?

When you look at it in this way, you can see that fear of failure is ridiculous. It seems overwhelming at times, yes. But it means nothing in the big scheme of things. So you may stumble and fall a few times. Big deal! Just get your backside in gear and get moving again! Failing is no fun. It feels bad. It will frustrate you for a while. But in the scope of life, what do most of your failures mean? Not much.

If the thought of failing is paralyzing you, you need to do an ego check. Who really cares if you fail? Name names. Your big, fat ego does not count. This may sound overly simple, but once you experience it for yourself, you realize how baseless a fear of failure really is.

Fear can be your end or it can be your beginning. If you decide fear is going to rule your decisions about how to succeed or not, then you won't. So hop in the recliner and watch old reruns. But if you decide that fear will be your motivator to overcome everything that may hold you back, then you will be on top in a short amount of time.

Doubt

Even if you do not fear success or failure, you might lack confidence in your own ability to overcome challenges and create the life you want. You might even doubt your ability to know the right path to take.

The only way to know for sure is to try! If you want to make positive changes in your life, you have to be willing to believe that you have what it takes. You have to believe that even if you do not initially have what it takes to succeed, you can work on developing it.

Do you think that any successful person was just born that way? Of course they weren't! All successful people have to go through a learning curve and continually push themselves past their limits. They had to start small and take one step at a time, honing their skills, developing new ones, and further strengthening those, too. You are no different.

Replace doubt about your ability to become successful with a belief that you can create the life and success you desire.

Success Actions That Work: If you cannot measure your progress over the past several months, you are not moving forward. You are resisting successful living in some way, and the time is now to start working through the things that are holding you back.

If what you have been doing has not worked, it is time to try something new. Instead of talking about it, do something. Identify what is blocking your success and then take steps to blast it the heck out of your life. You are already working hard at mediocrity and maintaining the status quo. Now it is time to start working hard at the success you truly want—and deserve.

5

Passion

Passion: (noun) Driving forces that compel us to act. This is not a singular term. You might want to think of it as passions.

Motivational author Napoleon Hill called this emotion "a burning desire." On the surface, that's an important part of passion. But there are far more components of passion than simply a burning desire.

Where do you see passion? Turn on the news. Take a look at the newspaper. Almost every headline. Almost every day.

Passion, of course, wires into all the *fears* in the brain as well as the drives. Example: One man perceives another man as a threat and adrenaline flows. The competitive (and sometimes deadly) nature of man kicks in. It becomes a focal point of consciousness, a point where nothing else matters. That's true passion.

Notice that the threat doesn't need to be real to invoke passion. Maybe the man didn't pose a real physical threat but a threat at work for a job, or to his relationship with his spouse, or to his intellect. But the first man's mind went where the fear was in his brain. How fascinating. The fear can be real or imagined but the ensuing behavior is powerful and passionate. Failure to keep that fear under complete control keeps doctors' offices and jails at capacity.

Where does passion come from? There are several sources.

Passion and your genes. Your genes are preprogrammed to try and keep you alive. They are preprogrammed to replicate. Those two things tell you much of what you need to know about the core of human behavior. Almost everyone has a passion to survive and participate in acts of replication so to speak. (Those who don't take themselves out of the gene pool quite quickly, as well as their potential future progeny.)

Passion and competition. Competition can fuel passion. Humans are by nature competitive. We compete in different ways. We compete for limited resources. We compete for glory. We compete physically, intellectually, and with force. We compete with ourselves. We compete with others . . . bring it on.

Passion and identity. People are passionate about their identities. You were born into an environment, typically a country or geographical unit that has a group identity. You also were born into a family, community, city, religion, and political orientation, all of which have identities that became part of you. You become passionate and emotion filled about the location where you live because it is part of your identity. You tend to like the people around you because of proximity and similarity or perceived threat from others. Your beliefs (religious, political, and societal) are all part of your identity, and you are passionate about these things when they become woven into your identity. You likely became passionate about most of these things for reasons that you did not choose.

Passion and choice. A unique part of your identity is formed from the choices you have made and will make about your life. These choices give you the only identity that you really control. For some people, the passions that come from the environment and family they were born into are enough to fuel a passionate life. But most people need to exercise their choice to develop new passions. This requires action. Fresh passion comes from creation. You will rarely find new passion by trying to "find yourself." It's difficult to find something if you haven't made a decision to put "it" in there. You need to recreate yourself.

Fresh passion can be powerful. Most often it develops when you are creating—building a house, writing a book, painting, making something that didn't exist before. It could be fueled by a new business or even a new job that suits your interests. Passion is about creating and then being proud of that creation, defending that creation, seeing it as an improvement on anything that has already been done.

Creation is where the burning desire is lit. The flames are fanned when you have invested yourself in the process of creation or growing or building and soon it becomes part of your identity. Then "it" becomes a front-page item in your life.

Once lit, the burning desire will do just that. It burns. It burns hot. There is no self-motivational affirmation that will make it grow hotter . . . or cool it down.

Passion is a unique and powerful factor of success. It is the fuel that provides forward thrust to the person who aspires to some level of greatness or achievement.

Question: I'm 45 years old and *still* don't know what I want to do when I "grow up." What's the best way to get this figured out?

You must be specific in identifying your passions. Then you must focus your efforts on that particular desire.

Here is the deal: When you have been in the same hamster wheel for a long time, you have no idea or dreams of what you want to be when you "grow up" . . . again.

You are by no means alone. The vast majority of people don't really know what they want. They haven't dreamed of what they want to be since high school. They thought the selection process was over when they got the job after high school or college.

For one moment they are excited over a particular thing or endeavor. The next thing you know they completely abandon it; either because they lose their interest or because they give up when they encounter a little problem. Those who always change their minds and those who give up easily when the going gets tough will not succeed.

Success Actions That Work: Maybe right now you are a bit confused. You don't seem to know what you really want in life. Consider these questions:

What is important to you?

What makes your heart beat with excitement?

What makes you happy?

What are you consistently thinking of day and night?

How would you spend your time if you didn't need to earn money?

What do you enjoy doing?

What have you always wanted to do?

What "music" do you have inside you that you want to get out before you die?

Now stop! Don't race past this. Do this . . . *now*. Just follow these three steps:

1. Write on a piece of paper all your possible answers for each of the questions above. Write anything, even seemingly unimportant ones.

2. Circle five to seven items that interest you the most.
3. Evaluate and choose with your heart the one or two things that are most worthy to spend all your time and resources on. The chosen one should be something that brings out the best in you.

Use your heart. Emotion is important at this stage. Why? Because early on in goal setting and motivation it is best to do something for which there will be little internal self-sabotage. You can always change later and dream new dreams.

In addition to the exercise above, ask your close friends and relatives how they see you and what they think you might be happy doing in the very near future. Other people often have a view of you that is far more accurate and prophetic than what you might see yourself. Also, look at the resources on Bestsuccessfactors.com for more guidance on figuring out your passions and establishing your direction.

The real answer to your question is this: *Do not go to sleep tonight without making a final decision on what you really want in life more than anything else!*

If you ignore this advice, then your dreams will end when you wake up. And that is no way to live.

Other people may offer comments or advice, but the final decision is always yours to make. Others may disagree with your decision. Let them. Be firm with what you really want. Ultimately, you should concentrate on what you want, not on what others want for you.

Once you know the activities that make your heart sing, throw yourself into them! Do them often and do them well. Master them like you've never mastered anything before. Become consumed by them.

When you do something you feel extremely passionate about, you automatically give the best of yourself to the task. You're not focusing on anything but the present moment, which means you are able to devote your full energy and attention to "now." You get in the flow.

When we are passionate about what we do, we end up enjoying ourselves to the fullest possible extent. We also lend that much more power to the end result. Focused, passionate action produces powerful results. So create something. Build something. Use your passion to make your unique contribution to the world.

Question: I get that it's important to follow my passions, but I have a long list of things each day that simply *must* get done. I have a job, family responsibilities, mundane chores, and all types of obligations. Not too glamorous and much of it lacks passion. How can I get more excited about my life?

We all have those things that simply have to get done. It's easy to slip into a mindset of drudgery and give only partial effort, and much of the time people do just that.

You can fuel your passion in everyday life by striving for and achieving personal excellence in everything you do. This creates a sense of inner pride about who we are and what we do. It makes us feel more confident, happier, and focused. Half-hearted effort leads to lukewarm results, but focused, full-effort action creates great results.

The first step toward creating more passion: *Commit to excellence in whatever you do.*

For example, don't clean out the garage because you "have to." Clean out the garage as if it were the most important thing you were doing that day. Clean it out as if a neat garage was of utmost importance in the grand scheme of things. Clean it out as if you would rather be doing nothing else in the world.

Are you questioning why your attitude really matters when cleaning out the garage? Let's look at what will happen if you approach any task with a sense of boredom or grudging obligation:

1. You won't enjoy the process at all. Your mind will be focusing only on getting it done, and you won't be giving your full attention to what you're doing. Consequently, you end up missing out on the enjoyment of the process. Even worse, you will be accustoming your brain to settling for less than your best effort in tasks you don't like to do. This is setting yourself up for disaster and will inevitably trip you up as you try to reach a higher level of success.
2. Because you didn't pay full attention to what you were doing, your results will be less than stellar. The garage might look okay and you rationalize that you are fine with that. But wouldn't "good" be better than "okay?" Sure, the garage doesn't need to be immaculate. It does need to be good and clean.
3. With a ho-hum attitude, you will miss out on that great sense of accomplishment and satisfaction that comes from a job done right.

Now let's take a look at what would happen if you began giving your mundane tasks your best effort and full attention:

1. You would find yourself feeling proud of your accomplishments and better about these unpleasant tasks. Rather than feeling annoyed or worn out by them, you'd begin to feel good about them. Sounds odd, but it is true.
2. You would start focusing more on the *benefits* created by the work you do, rather than the work itself.
3. You would gain a sense of personal mastery over just about everything you do. From errands to interpersonal relation-ships, each activity would feel like its own reward. The positive

results gained from undertaking these tasks would simply be a nice bonus—better organization, greater fulfillment, deeper relationships, and more powerful results from projects.

Success Actions That Work: It sounds as if you are focused more on getting each task done because it *needs* to be done. Throw yourself fully into those things that only you can do. If you want to experience more passion in your life, it makes sense that you would want to enjoy the things you do and experience better results from them. Giving greater effort also will help you get your chores done more quickly, freeing up more time to follow your bigger life passions.

Commit fully to everything you do. Focus your full attention on it and allow yourself to be immersed in the process. Give each task your absolute best and see how it dramatically enhances the result. Through this process, you will create more energy and passion for life!

Question: I went to a seminar that really stressed the importance of enthusiasm. How do we adopt that in our store? How do we encourage our employees to be enthusiastic when customers walk in? When they come to the counter? What's the best strategy?

People in retail are taught to approach the customer with a big smile and say, "Hi! Can I help you?" When they approach you with this question, you probably smile and say, "No thanks, I'm just looking." Or if you're like us you say something like, "No thanks, I'm beyond help . . . I'm just looking."

Similarly, in nonretail environments we're taught that we should be excited about our product and communicate that excitement in a contagious way to our prospects. For example, "I'm so excited about this new opportunity and once you try it you will be too!"

The reality is that a smile goes a long way but in most settings the giggly and bubbly emotions are not helpful. There are exceptions. Exaggerated emotion is expected in some contexts. But let's talk about the norm.

In the face-to-face sales world, an overexcited salesperson often will turn off a prospect. Using exaggerated emotion can feel artificial to others. If you fake it, you run the risk of coming on too strong and turning off far more people than you win over.

Success Actions That Work: A sound strategy is controlled enthusiasm.

The prospect doesn't want to see you bored with your product or service. Yet, if you sell pest control and flash a big smile and are overly upbeat and bubbly about getting rid of those bees or rats, the prospect is going to feel very uncomfortable.

Do this: Think about your product or service and how your client experiences it. What does the client get from using your product successfully? Whatever the appropriate response is to *that* question is the tone you want to adopt.

Example: You sell Avon perfume. When the prospect smells just perfect, the salesperson can get very upbeat and excited because that's how the prospect might feel. A little extra reinforcement can go a long way.

But let's say you sell cars. You don't need to get in the customer's face with enthusiasm and excitement. Smile when it makes sense. Keeping a smile plastered on your face invites doubt.

When you consider what your product or service or experience does for the client, it should give you a cluster of good feelings. Your product or service should generate a certain level of pride or excitement. Use these feelings as the benchmark for the level of enthusiasm you show to your clients and prospects.

Do not misunderstand. We are not saying that enthusiasm is a bad thing. But using it as an end in itself can easily backfire.

Controlled enthusiasm is not about ignoring the customer or prospect or being emotionless. You should be proud to sell your product. Exude that pride. You want to have a sense of certainty about your product where certainty is warranted. Just make sure that your level of enthusiasm is appropriate for your product or service.

6

Confidence

"I believe in myself!" Success gurus commonly have their followers chant this affirmation. And it is important to develop strategies that make you more aware of yourself and what you are capable of achieving. If you believe in yourself and your ability to achieve, then you are more likely to be successful in whatever you do.

But typically there are two important pieces left out of this type of belief affirmation. The first is action and the self-trust it creates. Believing in yourself means you are always persistent and that you always persevere. Period. If you don't, then your belief in yourself is worthless. If you don't do things that you promised yourself that you would do, you quickly learn not to trust yourself. Either you can do it or you can't. Either you get the job done or you don't. And your mind knows the truth.

Self-confidence is closely connected to self-discipline. Remember where we started? A recap: Self-discipline is not an attitude or a feeling. It is discipline. It is "do until." Greater self-discipline yields greater self-confidence and self-confidence in the correct proportions is a pillar of success.

The second piece that commonly is left out of the "believe in yourself" mantra is that confidence is a continuum. It is not that you either believe in yourself or you don't. The under confident end of the spectrum gets the most attention, but there are equal dangers on the other end.

The self-confidence continuum looks like this:

←Underconfidence—Confidence—

Certainty—

Overconfidence—Arrogance→

You don't want to be under confident. Research clearly shows that under confident people simply cannot achieve. Where there is little to no belief in the self, self-discipline never has an opportunity to engage.

You want to fall in the middle with a healthy dose of confidence and certainty. Self-confidence is a key predictor of success and income. To the degree you have self-confidence, you have a greater likelihood of becoming a higher income individual. Research shows that this is something that can be measured from childhood right to the paychecks the child will receive as an adult.

But what about the overconfident person? Research shows that these people often achieve for a brief period. And then they fail. High degrees of confidence are highly correlated with financial and relationship success. Overconfidence and arrogance are highly correlated with success and then failure.

We see this all of the time in sports. Look how often a football team is favored by 10 points and then loses or barely sneaks out a victory. What went wrong? This often results from a failure of overconfidence. In football, the overconfident get injured. They get beaten because they didn't put out 100 percent. They were taking it easy.

The great destroyer in reaching for achievement is arrogance and overconfidence. People who are too confident succumb to worse problems than people with little confidence. Confidence and overconfidence are two different worlds. Self-confidence is very important to achievement. Overconfidence can kill achievement.

Overconfidence in driving causes head-on collisions and can result in a car you cannot control when random events happen. Overconfidence in sex creates babies and spreads AIDS. Overconfidence in relationships destroys them. Overconfidence and arrogance in business leads to bad decisions, missed opportunities, and financial ruin.

There is a fine line between self-confidence (an absolute necessity for success) and arrogance. One wins. The other loses. Overconfident people cannot make it to the Super Bowl.

Every winning team in sports says this about their opponents, "They are a talented and tough team, and we will work hard to prepare for them." That is a positive mental attitude. That is the attitude of success.

Achievement is the result of the right mental attitude. Goliath should never overlook David. Goliath should never underestimate David. "We're going to win," is a very risky attitude.

As soon as you declare something that sounds like a fact, you'd better be right because your unconscious mind is listening. A confident attitude: "We know it is going to be tough but we will execute each play to the very best of our ability, and I believe we can and likely will win today." Be confident. But keep overconfidence and arrogance in check. Your mind is listening ... and it will show up in your behavior and in the results you produce.

Question: When you have lofty goals, you are put in a position where you really need to believe in yourself. I falter when I doubt myself. I try to fake it 'til I make it

but this only takes me so far. What can I do when I start doubting my ability to take the big steps that I really want to take?

Doubt, in the form of questioning, is necessary for success. Doubt is the birthing place of careful, concerned, and critical thinking. You must doubt your plan, those around you, how you are going to do things, and the entire process. You then go through each piece, analyze it, and become crystal clear on what is going to happen if (when) things go wrong.

But, it sounds like you doubt your ability to overcome difficulty. This is something that you must stop doing in order to succeed. This is a type of destructive doubt. It causes you to stand still when you'd rather be moving forward.

Destructive doubt can be sneaky, and it often masquerades as disinterest, bitterness, distrust, or resistance. It is a dream destroyer. It's the anti-hope. It causes you to abandon your dreams before you even know for sure if they're possible or not. You simply decide they are not possible and drop them.

If you seriously doubt your ability to do something, you won't do it. You won't even attempt it. Why would you?

If you doubt the availability of opportunities, you will resign yourself to what you already have. If you extend this doubt to the goodness of other people, you will resist any help offered to you.

In order to achieve, you need to take destructive doubt right out of the equation. You do this by embracing the opposite of destructive doubt, and that is constructive certainty or belief.

Constructive certainty is not arrogant. It is not overconfident. It is a belief that, once you have evaluated a situation and determined that something can be done, you are the person for the task. It is literally being certain of yourself.

Success Actions That Work: You have to make the decision to believe instead of doubt. This is a decision you will need to make not just once but over and over again. Every time you feel destructive doubt creeping in, replace it with fervent belief. You must construct certainty from evidence that you can indeed accomplish your task.

"I doubt I can do this effectively" becomes "I know I can do this effectively." (Then *act* on it.)

"I doubt it will turn out right" becomes "I'm going to make sure this turns out right." (Then *do* it.)

"I doubt I have what it takes to succeed" becomes "I know I can develop any quality I need to succeed." (Then *make it happen*.)

At first, you may feel as if you're lying to yourself. You may not really believe the words you're saying, but if you persist in constructing evidence and choosing to believe your outcomes, you will eventually win.

If fervent belief is not enough to eliminate your destructive doubts, you can also dissect them and challenge the underlying components. Take on the role of detective to figure out what is really going on inside of you. With a little scrutiny and a lot of brutal honesty, you will see things more clearly.

Fill in the blanks to complete the following statements:

"I am doubtful about _____ because _____."

"I am disinterested in _____ because I doubt that _____."

"I feel bitter about _____ because I doubt that _____."

"I'm distrustful of _____ because I doubt that _____."

"I'm resistant to _____ because I doubt that _____."

Dissection of any doubt is a valuable tool because the individual components that make up the sum are almost always less frightening than the sum itself. Once the root causes are known, you can deal with them one at a time by altering erroneous beliefs, facing fears, and expanding limiting beliefs.

You will likely discover that your destructive doubts are based on disappointing past experiences or hurtful things said by others in your life. You do have the option to disregard these completely. This is a choice.

Finally, if all else fails and you cannot eliminate or dissect your destructive doubt, the only thing left to do is ignore it. Take action anyway, even if it seems like a futile undertaking. With practice, you can skip all the other steps and move right to this stage. Don't think about it. Don't wonder about it. Just do it.

Here is a secret weapon: *Every time you even have a hint of doubt about your ability to overcome, immediately get to work on the project.*

Train your brain to respond to doubt with instant valuable action.

Make a promise to yourself that you are going to give your goals your absolute best no matter what. Even if it seems to be a waste of time, even if there seems to be no way to create a favorable outcome, and even if the going gets rough. You will still try. It takes courage and determination to do this. Do not fool yourself into thinking otherwise. But do not fool yourself into thinking it doesn't matter. It does.

Question: Do affirmations work? Will they help me become successful more quickly than if I don't use them?

The conventional wisdom is that affirmations are key to quickly making changes. Repeat what you want to create as if you are living it today and it will appear.

The hope is that we can think ourselves richer, healthier, happier, and more successful—all with little effort.

The results of using positive affirmations are mixed—some successes but certainly, they are no magic wand. Affirmations can be helpful if repeated often enough and for long enough. But inherent problems with random affirmations produce inconsistent results and they really are not very impressive in the final analysis.

A key problem is that when using positive affirmations, you try to get your mind to believe something that is generally quite a stretch from what it knows to be the truth.

Mind's reality: "I weigh 180 pounds."

Affirmative statement: "I weigh 120 pounds."

Until your mind accepts the affirmation as a statement of fact, the affirmation has very little power and can actually have a polarizing or opposite effect. When an affirmation runs up against your conscience, your unconscious mind knows you are not being truthful. The unconscious mind responds appropriately and finds a way to punish you, often through some self-sabotage mechanism. The brain is a pretty amazing thing.

Research shows that if you repeat something often enough and long enough, coupled with emotion, you probably will eventually believe it. So self brainwashing through affirmations can work ... if you get past the brain's defenses and self-sabotage.

A much more powerful method of changing beliefs is to use questions. Our brains are solution-finding machines. They solve problems and feel compelled to answer questions presented to them.

The difference between how the brain responds to statements and to questions is profound. When you use an affirmative statement, you are simply trying to convince yourself that something is true when in reality it is not. You're "lying" to yourself and that can create all kinds of problems in the mind.

When you use questions, specifically positive affirmative questions, you are setting in motion the mechanism for your brain to find and focus on the solution and enter into a reprogramming cycle to seek and believe things that are positive and useful to you.

Here are some examples:

Affirmation	Positive Affirmative Question
"I feel good."	"How can I feel good about myself?"
"I feel good about myself."	"Why do I feel good about myself?"
"I like myself."	"What do I like about myself?"
"I like myself just the way I am."	"What can I change about myself so I like myself more?"
"I am successful."	"Why am I becoming more successful?"
"I am successful just the way I am."	"What can I do to make myself more successful?"

Can you see the difference?

An affirmation has an inherent artificiality. It feels fake and puts you in a position of being incongruent. A question, on the other hand, is investigative. It's motivating in and of itself. It's a real, honest, self-validating motivational strategy for achievement.

Saying, "I feel good" or "I feel good about myself" can be effective if there's some truth in the statement. If you already feel good or at least okay, the positive statements will reinforce and heighten the good feeling. But, if you are feeling bad or depressed, you will struggle to change your mood simply by repeating, "I feel good," because you are trying to convince your mind of something it knows is not true.

Have you ever tried to change someone's beliefs just by repeatedly stating the opposite? It is hard work!

Affirmative questions are much more powerful. When you ask yourself, "How can I feel good about myself?" you are not trying to convince yourself of something you know is not true. Instead, you are asking your mind to look for a positive and useful answer. This will quickly change your focus and is the surest route to changing your feelings from negative to positive.

The question, "Why do I feel good about myself?" is especially powerful because not only is it a question programming your mind to seek out reasons to feel good, but it also contains the positive statement that you feel good.

Another affirmative statement from above is: "I am successful just the way I am." Use caution with these types of affirmations. This type of statement actually can diminish your motivation and drive to improve. If you are convinced you're successful just the way you are, you have no reason to better yourself and move forward. You can get stuck.

The affirmative question, "What can I do to make myself more successful?" does the exact opposite. By using the word "more," the question implies that you are already a success in some way, and then it programs your mind to focus on using its enormous power to identify ways you can become even more successful.

Success Actions That Work: Convert any affirmations you are currently using into positive affirmative questions. Dig deeper and ask yourself, "What powerful questions can I ask myself today to change my life for the better?" Make a list. And use it. We predict that if you use positive affirmative questions for a couple of months and track your experiences, you will see some substantial steps toward greater success.

Question: **Sometimes I find myself frozen and unable to take action. My mind gets that I need to "just do it!" But that's not always enough to convince my body to move forward and take the risks. How can I convince myself to go and do when I feel like I can't?**

First, you need to convince yourself that there is no actual danger. (And do be sure that you are correct!) It is your belief that something will go horribly wrong if you move forward that keeps you locked in terror.

One simple way to overcome this paralysis is to ask yourself, "What is the worst thing that could happen?" And, "Could I handle it if the worst did happen?" Most often, you will come to see that you can handle things should they go as badly as you are afraid they might.

Second, plan ahead so you know what to do if the worst happens. If your fear is public speaking but you really want to (or have to) give a speech, ask yourself what the worst possible occurrence might be if you go ahead. You might answer, "stage fright," or "forgetting what I want to say." Consider how you would handle those situations. Could you work off of notes if you need to? Could you laugh it off and turn the moment into a joke for the audience? Would it help to visualize the audience members in their underwear? You get the idea ... turn your worst-case scenario into a "so what?" and your perspective will change.

Third, script a different outcome in your mind. Whatever your feared outcome is, come up with an inner script that is in direct opposition to it. Replay this script over and over in your mind until you believe it. Using the public speaking example, visualize yourself feeling pumped up, dynamic, and confident as you step onto the stage. See the audience being interested in what you have to say, listening closely, laughing at the appropriate moments, and your words flowing smoothly and effortlessly. Imagine the thunderous applause as you conclude your speech, and imagine the incredible sense of elation you'll feel for conquering your fear.

Fourth, shrink your fears so you can crush them. Fears tend to feel so much bigger than they are. It feels like they loom over you, draining your power and diminishing your determination. Change this perception by imagining your fears shrinking, shrinking, growing smaller and less intense until they are no bigger than a bug on the ground before you. Tell the fear that you are grateful for its attempt to protect you, but you do not need protecting. Then ... if you like ... step on it. Squash it into oblivion.

There are many more ways to challenge your fears, but the main point is to avoid letting them control your life. Fear can be so pervasive that it seems to be out of our control, but remember that a fear is nothing more than a feeling. Whether you examine it closely, question it, challenge it, work calmly through it, or push forcefully through it doesn't matter. As long as you remember that you are the one in control, not your fears.

Here is a secret: Fear makes you think that the top is much farther away than it is!

For years, philosophers and writers have found eloquent ways to say this: Just when it seems that you cannot hold on a minute longer, hold on tighter because the tide is about to turn. This sentiment has been repeated because it is true. The irony about progress is that right when you think you cannot go a step farther, you are often much closer to the finish line than you think. It is your own thoughts, fears, doubts, beliefs, and expectations that make the destination seem so small and far away. If you buy into this illusion, you will give up in the homestretch—not realizing that the finish line is just over the next hill!

Success Actions That Work: Your challenge is to learn how to push yourself to move forward when everything within you is screaming in panic. Let us tell you that people do this everyday. We have coached thousands of people to successfully do this. *You can do this.*

There is no magic moment in the way you likely have been thinking there is. You find yourself hanging back, waiting for just the right moment to move on something you want to do. You know you want to move forward. You are practically chomping at the bit ... but something holds you back. You are waiting for your confidence to reach a certain level so you will feel ready. In other words, you do not believe that you already have the ability to succeed at your objective.

Obviously if you are waiting for your confidence to hit a level that you have not experienced before, then a powerful circular behavioral loop is going to occur. You will never take action. As you said, *you can't*. Why? Because you will not know when you have enough confidence. There is no way to measure it to convince yourself that you are ready to go. With all the technology out there, we have yet to see a confidence thermometer (confidometer?).

The magic moment you have been waiting for ... is *NOW*.

People get so used to comfort zones and mundane routines. Trying to do something new makes just about everyone feel uneasy until they become comfortable with it. Fear is simply a result of feeling out of your element. Use the techniques above to push past that initial fear, and you will realize that there really is nothing to fear. You also will find that walking through your fear will quickly lead to a higher level of achievement and greater success.

7
Mastering Criticism

Why do kids quit or fail to achieve? Think about it. They initially fail at walking, talking, manners, riding a bike, playing a game, making decisions, reading, adding, subtracting—everything. There is nothing a child gets right the first time.

How the parents and the people in the environment deal with that chronic failure (learning experiences) is, in large part, going to shape that child's potential for success.

"If at first you don't succeed try, try again." Did your mom or dad get that one right? If so, you are a lucky one.

Some parents chose to say things like this:

"You will never get it right."

"You are learning disabled, don't worry about it. No one expects you to do a good job."

"You can't do anything right, can you?"

If you heard phrases like these, they were destructive. In large part these statements and the reactions they triggered in you determined your success (or lack of it) as a young adult. Are they still affecting you today?

To avoid criticism, some people stay within their comfort zone or they do precisely what is anticipated and they simply get no negative feedback. People who don't want to get criticized never do anything they don't already know how to do because they don't want to fail. Yet, people who rarely get criticized ultimately fail. Don't fall into this trap.

You work, you love, you play. And you get criticized. It hurts and is embarrassing. That is the real world and you need to accept it in order to excel in it.

No matter the root, criticism hurts a little, hurts a lot, or is excruciating. Can you ever recall a time when someone came straight out with criticism and you said, "Oh yeah, man do I feel better now!" It's not going to happen. We're just like you. We don't like criticism (even constructive criticism), and we don't like rejection.

So just how do you deal with criticism?

First, you have to feel your emotions as you hear the criticism. Don't fight back. Don't shout. Don't scream. Don't leave blood-stains. Breathe. Next, you have to step back from the emotion and determine three things:

1. Was the critic correct in his assessment?
2. Did the critic intend to cause you pain?
3. Do you care about the critic as a person?

Accuracy first. Was he even close to right? Is it possible the evaluation of you or your work has any merit at all? Even a little? If not, it's unwarranted and it isn't criticism, it's jerkism.

Next you have to determine if the person was criticizing you as a person or whatever it was you did. For example, the critic did not like your painting. But, is he saying that you are a bad artist because your painting isn't so great or is he saying *this* painting isn't so hot? How wide has the net been set? Criticism by people who throw wide nets is rarely worth listening to.

Finally, does the critic truly care about you as a person and do you care about him? People who love us criticize us every day. Criticism from people who don't shouldn't register on our radar. It's not that the loved one is more accurate. In fact, loved ones tend to be biased against each other in their criticism. But the value of the relationship makes the criticism worth exploring. The criticism of someone who doesn't care is not worth wasting your time on.

If several people in your life have mentioned that you seem to lack purpose or confidence, or you're too timid, abrasive, shy, arrogant or any other unflattering description, ask yourself why they might have this impression of you. If the critic is correct (or close), then try to look at the painful communication as useful. No matter how useful, criticism will always sting. Everyone hates being told they are wrong or lacking in some way.

The reality is that criticism is common along the road to success and most of it is meaningless. When someone has made the decision to start a business or make a change in his life or put himself out in public in some way, criticism is going to follow. Do not give your energy to it or let it stop you in your tracks. Never allow criticism to de-motivate you.

If you want to succeed, you are implicitly asking to be criticized. Accept this as part of your path to success. Because criticism can feel so painful, very few people will choose the path that has critics on it. Therefore, the path to achievement is generally a very clear road to travel if you can handle the feelings of rejection and criticism. And, you can!

No one can achieve at a high level if they can't cope in some way with criticism. The greater the number of people you will be seen by, the more you will be criticized. Successful people use criticism as leverage to excel and do better, make a better product, improve service, and make more money. Never again let criticism stand in between you and achievement.

Question: **I'm in a fairly high profile position (in the public a lot). I seem to get criticized from all sides—including at live events and in the local press. I have stopped reading the newspaper articles where I'm featured. What else can I do to not let this constant criticism get under my skin?**

Face it. When one person writes or speaks about you in a critical way, someone else was thinking the same thing. You are in good company. American presidents rarely garner more than 50 percent of the votes when winning a election. The fact is that the more people know you, the greater the number of people who will criticize you. This is reality. When you are in the public eye, you cannot escape criticism.

That said, if you continue to listen to your loudest critic, you will fail. Whatever your professional position, your goal is not to please everyone. It's not even to please 50 percent of the people. Your goal is to serve your audience. It is to be your customers' servant. It is to be your friends' friend. It is to be true to yourself.

In business, the most valuable criticism you receive is from those people whom you serve, consult with, or are your most loyal customers. Pay close attention to these voices. They have your best interests at heart just as you have theirs at heart.

When you hear criticism from your customers and clients, you must listen. That does not mean they are right. It means no such thing. It means you listen. When possible, you make the person who criticized you a hero.

You need criticism to succeed. The only way you can never be criticized is to do nothing.

Why are you a target? People tend to criticize when they don't like what you've done for whatever reason and they feel compelled to tell you. There are a lot of possible reasons for the criticism.

Sometimes people think they are teaching you something.

Sometimes they want to feel superior to you.

Sometimes they want to help you.

Sometimes they care about you and don't want you to look bad to others.

People often criticize when they feel their self-esteem threatened. They compare themselves to you and realize that they don't want to discipline themselves to achieve what you have. They criticize to make themselves feel better. It's their idea of unconscious justice.

It sounds like the criticism you receive is more personal in nature. We feel your pain. Each of us is a professional public speaker who speaks before audiences all over the world about everything from sales to negotiation to body language to motivation to leadership. Thousands and thousands of people . . . and sometimes there are people somewhere in the audience that have had a very bad day.

Maybe someone died in their family. Maybe they got yelled at by a spouse. Maybe they got a demotion. Who knows? They vent. They take their pain out on you. It's like playing football. If you don't ever want to get hit, then don't put on a football uniform. If you do, you are going to get hit.

Success Actions That Work: When people criticize in public, it can be particularly painful. If the complaint is valid, then make the changes necessary. If it's not, feel free to appreciate their point of view and share yours and thank them for their feedback. It rarely makes sense to argue or debate your critic. Once people state their opinions publicly, will they change their minds? Of course not! But if the criticism is unwarranted, other people will almost always disagree with the person criticizing you. Focus your efforts on these supporters.

When conversing with a critic, you can buffer the criticism by taking the focus off a singular negative and split screening it with an experience that was positive.

Criticism: "I didn't like your last book."

Internal response: "You have no clue. We worked endless hours putting that together and it's the best book on the subject you'll ever read."

External response: "Which book in this area have you liked best, and what was it about it that made it special?"

Connecting a negative with a positive in this way can reduce unnecessary hard feelings.

Criticism disquiets all of us, but it need not destroy us. Accept this as a reality of life—especially a life lived in public. Never, ever let criticism stand between you and achievement.

Question: One of my coworkers constantly makes negative comments about me, my work, and my choices. I usually see this coming because she says, "Don't take it personally but . . ." and then unloads on me. I do take it personally. Am I being too sensitive?

Oh, that common disclaimer made when negative or insulting comments are about to be shared. Don't take it personally. . . .

You may be tempted to try and dismiss negative comments simply because they conflict with the image you would like to have of yourself. While you can't mindlessly believe everything a person says about you either, you might want to selectively absorb pieces of information and use them as fuel for motivation.

There are three possibilities about negative comments or negative feedback:

1. The feedback is mostly accurate and you should use it to motivate change in yourself.
2. The feedback is mixed in its accuracy and you should use it to make change where it is needed.
3. The feedback is a lot of garbage and you should ignore it or, better yet, use it to drive yourself to greater success.

If your coworker is the only person who feels the way she does, then her comments probably don't hold merit. But if several people all seem to have the same impression of you, there may be something worth looking at there. Think about these comments objectively and ask yourself whether they might contain a grain of truth.

It is possible that all of her criticism is unjustified. Unwarranted criticism comes from the same family as cruelty and violence. Each is a differently sized apple on the same tree. People really can be mean. People across the world lose their lives everyday because group A wants group B to be like group A. When group B chooses to not be like group A, violence can result. Understanding this is important at every level of your life.

People have a strong bias that causes them to think that they are right and that the other person is wrong. This bias commonly manifests itself on the field that you play on in business and in life. If your coworker's comments highlight areas of your performance, personality, or habits that truly could use some improvement, use the feedback you've received to make positive changes in your life. If your critic is way off-base, then remind yourself that her comments are really about her, not you.

Success Actions That Work: Make a list of the unflattering things that your coworker and other people have said to you (this exercise also works for negative things that you frequently say to yourself.) Then go down the list and honestly assess whether they hold merit. Some of them won't, and you can cross those off the list. The others, however, hold a big key to your personality—and you are in control of those things!

Remember just because five people say you are "X" doesn't mean you *are* X. It doesn't mean that they are right. It does mean that they either see you or want to see you as an X, and this is valuable information for you to have.

If you want to achieve, be prepared for some people to want you to fail. Your coworker might be one of these people. You'll know you're starting to become successful when you hit the radar screen of detractors. So take heart. If you're putting up with criticism (especially unwarranted criticism), you must be doing a lot right.

If it becomes clear that you are dealing with a negative person whose sole intent seems to be to suck the life out of you, you do have a *choice* to not engage.

Stop! We have heard all of the excuses. The most common ones are, "I have to work with this person," or "but they are my family." You do not *have* to work with anyone, you *choose* to. You do not *have* to interact with anyone, you *choose* to. Direct confrontation often is effective. Tell your coworker that you find her behavior distracting and ask her to stop what she is doing. Find new ways to prevent this type of interaction by deciding ahead of time what alternative actions you will take instead of dealing with her in a destructive way. If needed, ask yourself, "How can I appropriately and ethically move this person out of my life?"

If you decide to keep a critical person in your life, then we advise you to take this type of comment literally. When you hear, "Don't take this personally . . ." then *don't* take it personally. Refuse to expend your energy dealing with whatever venom next spews from her mouth. Better yet, use her critical words as rocket fuel to propel you to achieve something great that you would not otherwise have done.

Question: As a manager, I frequently am involved in resolving conflict. Sometimes I am a party to that conflict, and sometimes it involves others. I understand the importance of taking the high road, but it's a lot easier said than done. Any advice to keep things running smoothly and keeping my team on track?

It is easy to get caught up in workplace conflict, especially if it is being fueled by someone who thrives off drama. Take a step back and ask yourself a few questions.

What Behavior Needs to Be Changed?

Focus on behaviors and not people. Focusing attention on individuals, especially when they are defensive, can quickly lead to more conflict. A defensive person is likely to interpret personal feedback, even when well intended, as really saying, "this is all your fault."

Maintaining a focus on issues and observable behaviors makes the situation less threatening. It is also helpful to specify the desired behavior and give nonpersonal reasons why a change in behavior will be good for the team.

What Are the Facts?

Focus on facts and not judgments. Facts are objective. Although some people will still try to argue over facts, they are least likely to be the source of conflict. Judgments, on the other hand, are subjective. Two people can easily differ and argue about whose judgment is the better one.

What's the difference between a comment based on fact and a judgment? A fact uses an objective or measurable standard: "We need you here by 8:00, yet you arrived at 8:15 on Monday and 8:23 on Thursday." A judgment uses a personal point of reference: "You are always late for work."

The distinction between fact and judgment highlights why using "I statements" helps support positive communication. The statement, "You are disrespectful," is a judgment while, "I felt that your statement was disrespectful," is a fact. Reporting how you feel instead of judging the other person or their intent can help de-escalate conflict and keep your conversation on a positive note.

Can You Agree to Disagree?

This might be the best that you can do in a situation. And it's okay. If the disagreement at issue does not materially affect the task or project you're working on, then agree to simply take it off the table and be nice to each other.

People can reasonably have different judgments or opinions about what is the best action in any given situation or what the implications might be. If you are willing to live with some disagreement, without personally being disagreeable (this is the secret and the challenge!), you often can maintain a good working relationship.

Can You Be a Hero and Take One for the Team?

Yes, taking the high road is a good strategy. Look at your intentions. When possible, adopt a mind-set of yielding as needed for the greater good.

When neither side agrees to budge, it can undo an entire project or team. No clear winner can emerge from this type of stalemate.

Each party can convince itself that it is right, but try taking that to the bank. This type of impasse only creates losers.

Someone needs to step up, be a hero, and take one for the greater good. Why not you?

A willingness to yield and help both parties get most of what each one wants requires a high level of leadership. Work on developing this type of maturity, both as a manager and as an individual.

We often see that when one party shows a *willingness* to yield, it often eliminates the need to actually yield. Simply showing personal integrity and a willing intent can change the tone of the interaction and be enough to bridge the gap between the conflicting positions.

Success Actions That Work: Stick to observing behaviors and focusing on the facts. If you disagree about the facts of a situation, actively seek to create a common understanding of them. You then can work toward understanding each other's subjective judgments.

If you reach an impasse on certain points of disagreement, try to respectfully agree to disagree and keep moving forward. Finally, you will work toward resolution most quickly if you display an honest willingness to yield to the other's position. Even if you do need to give a little, the payoff is that your energy can be directed toward progress rather than wasted in exhausting and nonproductive conflict.

Question: **It's really important to me what other people think of me—sometimes too important. Wondering what someone thinks about what I've done or said can keep me up at night. How can I balance using feedback from others to make improvements without putting too much weight on others' opinions?**

Being susceptible to the opinions of other people can be a *huge* obstacle to achievement. To be successful, you need to determine whose opinions matter to you and whose do not.

Are we saying that you shouldn't listen to advice from other people? No, not at all. But you have to consider the source. Is the advice legitimate? On what knowledge or experience is it based? Do you have a new set of information on which to test it? You must decide what to do based on the real information at hand, not the prejudices and concerns of other people.

There are some people whose opinions need to matter to you, such as the person who hires you, the person who signs your check, and your life partner. You don't live alone on the planet, but you sure don't have to live in fear of other people's opinions of you.

As we talk about in more detail when we address support structures, you need to select a handful of people whose opinion you will seek out and consider. Search out people who will disagree with you, challenge you, and call you out when you do stupid stuff that will get in the way of your success. You want a group of advisors, mentors, and coaches to kick you in the butt, in a direction you've asked them to kick, even when you don't feel like being kicked. This is not the type of opinion giving that we are talking about here.

Putting too much weight on other people's opinions is a monster-sized problem we see with a majority of success-minded individuals. It affects the way they approach achievement, motivation, their individual goals, and desired lifestyle. It is extremely important to be able to tell most of the world that you don't care what it thinks while you go on the life journey that *you* have designed.

If you are held back by lack of action, timidity, fear of failure, or any other issue that may cause you embarrassment or ridicule, then you have a problem with caring more about other people's thoughts than about your success.

Think about your finances. Do you give in to going out when you know you don't have the cash? Do you make big, expensive purchases to make sure you don't look like the "outsider" while all the while your money situation is totally out of control? Then you care too much what others think.

You need to decide. What do you want?

Are you trying to succeed in your career by earning a promotion?

Do you want to lose weight?

Do you dream of building wealth?

Do you desire a great relationship?

Do you want to write a book?

If you let the value you place on the opinions of other people get in your way, you won't accomplish any of these things. You must recognize how much power you are giving away to the opinions of others.

People who are more inclined to say no than yes and who are unwilling to take chances of their own to achieve their dreams are not valid detractors. And here is the thing. Most of the people who would hold you back are holding you back because of their fears not your own. Their fear is so strong that they project it onto you to fulfill their need to stay afraid. If you succeed where they fear or where they fail, their fear and failure feels even more pronounced. And people who would abandon you for making a decision that they would not make are not really friends so their opinion shouldn't matter, anyway.

Success Actions That Work: Here are some things you can do to stop caring too much about what others think.

1. Define Yourself

You must define yourself. As Shakespeare said, "To thine own self be true." If you are not being true to yourself, the road to success will be difficult.

Here are some questions you can answer to develop a solid sense of self. Answer them after, and only after, you really think about them.

What is your value?

Can you truly achieve success in business, life, relationships, and other areas? What does this success look like?

Do you believe in yourself enough to be able to carry out purpose-centered goals?

Once you have developed a better sense of self, you must do what you would if you wanted to master anything else. You must practice. You must constantly be aware of who you are, what you are doing, and why you choose to act or react in any given situation. Are you choosing your behavior or is it dictated by what others may think?

You will not fulfill your destiny without knowing who you are. You will not reach your destiny without being true to yourself.

2. Take a Stand

There is an old saying, "If you don't stand for something, then you'll fall for anything." This is a profound statement. Think about it. The fact is if you don't stand up for your convictions and your passions, you'll wimp out and fold when you are challenged.

Take a stand. Know *why* you take a stand. Know your position on what you believe and know why you take that position. Do not just believe something because you heard it somewhere and your friends seem to believe it. You are too valuable as an individual to be someone else's parrot.

Be an individual and you will make a powerful impression.

3. Take Directed and Continuous Action

When you have firmly claimed your passions and convictions to the point you will fight for them no matter who differs in opinion, you are ready to take massive action toward your goals, desires, and dreams. The hardest part will be growing the backbone to stand up for your convictions (especially if you don't have that type of personality). But once you have reached that point, it becomes easier to aggressively pursue your dreams.

In fact, no one will seriously get in your way. You will find more people who are willing to help you get to where you want to go than will stand in your way.

Why?

Because you will be living the life you are meant to live. You will be passionate about what you believe. You will indirectly command respect and you will eventually find a following. You will find a following because most people don't know what they believe and they jump at the first opportunity to follow a passionate, firmly rooted individual. And once you've begun your journey and are moving forward, you'll begin to build momentum.

The solution to caring too much about what others think takes effort and practice. But you can make changes within your mind to make it happen. And the result is that you'll have much more self-respect—and respect from others—about your achievements. Begin to make this investment in yourself today.

8

Self-Control

Self-control is the ability to make decisions about how and when we express our thoughts and feelings, and which of our impulses to act on.

Control means you take 100 percent responsibility for doing everything you can to generate an outcome. It does not mean you have 100 percent control. No one has that much control over life.

Bad things happen and they happen a lot. You can't alter the course of the storm. You can only maneuver through it in such a way that allows you and those you love to survive and then thrive when the storm passes.

Self-control is about driving your own brain as you would a car.

You think of where you want to go.

You head out in that direction.

Stuff happens along the way (like detours and road construction).

You either wait for the road to open (next year) or take a detour now.

You check to see if you're getting there using the new route.

You get there.

You achieved your destination because of self-control.

In the last 20 years, self-control or self-regulation has become a hot topic of scientific study. Social scientists are exploring what it takes to be in control of the self. We are learning more and more about what works and what does not.

So why do people find themselves completely unable to reroute their plans and control or direct their frustrations toward changing their behaviors to get to their destination? Why do they seem to prefer to just get somewhere, which is right next to nowhere? It's because they never learned to self-regulate.

Without self-control, you will not be able to keep in check all the self-destructive and irrational behaviors that can take you off the path of success. For example, one form of self-regulation is not getting caught up in perfectionism. Top achievers understand that it doesn't really matter if the detour sign reads "deture." All they care about is *using* the detour route to get to where they want to go while everyone else gets sidetracked trying to find someone to fix the misspelling.

Spending time thinking about what to do with the "deture" sign brings you how much fulfillment? Money? Happiness? Zip. Practicing self-control and staying on task, figuring out how to use the "deture" to get where you want to go does bring fulfillment, money, and happiness. Big difference.

Strengthening self-control is an everyday, lifelong process, which starts from today and (we hope) continues for the rest of your life.

Let's do a quick visualization that will help you better grasp the concept of self-control. Imagine that you are reading this book resting in a cozy chair. You are totally relaxed, warm and comfortable. You are enjoying it.

Suddenly a phone rings.

What do you do? Of course you answer it.

Do you know why you answer the phone when it rings? Not because you are expecting some life-changing news or because you can't wait to see who's calling. You answer the phone due to your previous conditioning. The ring of the phone is a signal, an irritant, that you have learned to obey. You do it without thinking or making any special decision. A phone rings—you react. You get up from your comfortable chair, put your book aside, and hurry to answer it.

From a logical, pragmatic, nonconditioned point of view, if you are not dealing with a crisis or need to be available for a particular person, then why would you completely disrupt what you are doing to answer the phone?

Do you see how easily that external irritant has set you in motion? It has changed your previous mind-set and course of action. After all, you were planning on reading in peace and quiet for some time. You were looking forward to it. Unfortunately, your deeply conditioned reaction to this irritant has ruined your beautiful plans.

This is a simple everyday example designed to help you pay attention to one little detail that most of us so often forget: You did not have to react in any way to the ringing phone. You could have totally ignored it. Instead of getting up, you could have been relaxing and letting your body soak into that comfortable chair. All you had to do is to stick to you initial plan, read, rest, learn—all on purpose, all with intention.

Then you let someone else start driving your brain. You got right up out of the chair and said, "Hey, the phone is ringing. That means it's time for me to now stop controlling myself and let some random person drive my brain."

Now imagine the same situation but a slightly different scenario. You are enjoying yourself, reading, learning, and letting your mind and body rest. The phone rings. But instead of getting up, you ignore the phone and continue to focus on your book. In the back of your mind you are aware of the sound that your phone is making, but you are not paying any attention to it. You refuse to follow your initial reflex. The phone doesn't have any control over your behavior and cannot move you an inch.

This is the type of self-control exerted by top achievers. They turn off the ringer ... or curse themselves for not turning the ringer off and then let the phone ring a few times before it goes to voice mail.

Do not misunderstand. There is nothing wrong with picking up the phone. We're not saying that you should never answer the phone again. (If your relative is in the hospital or your kids are in school and you anticipate their call for some reason, go get the phone.) But this example shows how often we are hijacked into the habit of reacting in a certain way to the different stimuli coming from the outside. We do it without even thinking or giving it a backward glance. You need to condition yourself to hear a phone ring and be able to ask yourself, "Who would I want to talk to?" Look at the caller ID. Is that person on the other end?

Exerting self-control takes practice. It is very hard at first not to answer the phone. You feel weird. You feel guilty. You feel like you might be missing something. You feel all kinds of negative emotions. But you can choose to ignore the phone and simply let it ring.

Worry, anger, and anxiety are almost always a cause of overreaction of your body's alarm signals. By learning how to ignore a ringing phone, you are creating an internal tranquilizer. You create a psychological barrier between an irritant and yourself. By practicing delaying your habitual response, you are protecting yourself from overreacting and reducing your conditioned reflexes.

The same principle works for nearly all stress-inducing situations. This doesn't mean that you can ignore real problems. No, you'll still have to deal with any real problem requiring a reaction or response from you. But, you have to learn to respond from an emotionally neutral place where your mind is as clear and calm as possible. When you act under stress, your mind is anxious, your nervous system is strained, and you will make a poor decision.

Self-control is about changing conditioned responses formed over the past decades and taking charge of the situation. You can control yourself. You can choose to stay calm when facing a problem or situation. Top achievers stay in control of themselves, their emotions, and any situation in which they find themselves.

Question: **I've been known to give a knee-jerk reaction to situations at work. I'm trying to work my way up to management and know I need to get this tendency under control. Can you offer any advice on how to stay cool when someone else is really pushing my buttons?**

With predictability, other people will try to mess up your day. Some people love to do this on a regular basis because they are reaction addicts. They do what they think they need to do to feel good in the moment. And how do you feel when others do stuff to mess up your day? Angry ... frustrated ... depressed ... anxious? This does not need to be your experience. If you are going to pick an emotion, how about feeling disappointed that they are missing out on life?

Or better yet, learn to detach from emotion before responding. To be successful as a manager or in any other area of your life, you need to master self-regulation. You will make better decisions and have more positive interactions with others when you emotionally detach. This will keep your mind as clear as possible.

Self-control is a concept that sounds easy, but it is not. You know how hard it can be to keep your mind at ease when other people are messing with you or you are put in stressful situations. This is especially true when you are unprepared and caught off guard. In these situations, how do you exercise self-control?

Here are some proven strategies to help you stay in control:

Delay your reaction. When you learn to delay your reaction to a stressor, you are breaking a habit-forming cycle of an immediate, explosive reaction. You probably have heard the simple advice to count to 10 when you need to calm down. Counting to 10 is a way of delaying your reaction. It is quite useful on one condition. You need to count very *slowly*. You are effectively procrastinating your reaction. Counting to 10 will take your mind out of an explosive situation, while you back off and help release some muscle tension.

Control your breathing. Oftentimes, the most important step is to take control of your breathing. On a physical level, steady breathing slows the heart rate into a smooth beat and oxygen is delivered in a regular supply to the brain and around the entire body. Breathe deeply and slowly from your diaphragm (your belly, not your chest.) Breathing for even 10 seconds before reacting can be a big step toward reducing your conditioned reflexes and creating new ones.

Get creative. Music has long been shown to be a powerful relaxation tool. Use this to your advantage by playing a relaxing CD when you are in a stressful environment. Recent research shows that humming a song or making the type of sound generally associated with meditation ("hmmmmm") helps disrupt the stress cycle. Relaxing your jaw muscle, where you tend to carry a lot of tension, also can help. Even chewing gum has been shown to improve your ability to handle stressful situations. New research continues to be released on effective stress management techniques and some of these findings may surprise you. Read up on these latest techniques, keep an open mind as you experiment with them, and find what works best to get you back in control of the situation.

Take one thing at a time. In reality, most of our emotional problems come from an inability to be comfortable in a situation as it is. The one thing in life that you can successfully change and control is yourself. So respond emotionally only to a problem that exists here and now, leaving everything else aside. Concentrating on one aspect of a situation at a time can help you to solve your problem more easily in a step-by-step fashion.

Listen. For two people to communicate clearly, there needs to be a talker and a listener. However, in an argument there are two talkers and no listeners. Thus, to resolve and avoid expanding an argument, listen to the other person. Even if they are wrong, don't let your emotions take control. Do not hold others to artificially high and unrealistic standards. No one is perfect. Accept that and listen respectfully.

Visualize yourself calm. Irritated or angry people tend to jump to lousy conclusions, blaming everything and everyone and exaggerating the worst of the situation. Slow down and think carefully about what you want to say. You may offend someone and regret it two seconds later. Practice visualizing situations from the past when you've lost control and over-reacted ... but now picture yourself staying calm and acting with dignity. Rewrite your experiences in your mind so that you can better rewrite them in reality.

Create a safe place. Security feeds a feeling of control. You will more efficiently handle situations when you feel protected and safe. When you build in the space you need to better choose your response to a situation, you will feel more confident and be less likely to immediately react without thinking.

But where do you go to get away from the initial emotions caused by a situation? You can't just storm out of the room in the middle of the workday. You can't always find time for a vacation. Where do you find security to make a reasoned decision in the midst of your stressful, hectic life?

Top achievers create their own refuge. In the last months of the Second World War, one journalist asked President Truman how he was seemingly able to handle all the difficulties and tensions of his presidential duties more easily than his predecessors. How did he appear to exude such youthful energy during such hard times? Truman's secret was simple in its geniality. He explained that he had created a peaceful place in his imagination, where he would retire every time he needed to relax and regain strength. It was a place where he could get away from all the worries and problems.

We all need that kind of place, and it is possible. With practice, it only takes a few minutes to find that shelter and create a change of scenery in our imagination. Like the deepest part of an ocean, your imaginary shelter stays unmoved and undisturbed even by the strongest storms.

Here is an example of how to create your refuge. Imagine a nice, cozy room. Paint the walls in serene colors (blue, green, lavendar, or gold). See the room as clean and organized. This will give you a sense of clarity and help you clear your head. A big, comfortable inviting chair is a must! Imagine looking out of the window. What do you see? A sandy beach? Waves slowly moving in and out over the warm sand, seagulls flying high in the air. It is peaceful and quiet. The key here is to make it look as realistic as possible.

When you are creating your safe place, pay great attention to the details. Build a place where you really like spending time. Scientists have found that specific images (especially if they have a symbolic meaning to us) have a greater influence on our nervous system than do words. Begin spending 5 to 10 minutes a day in your inner haven and work up to 20 minutes. This is a good use of time. You will be giving yourself the space and time you need to get back in control of your emotions and choose an appropriate response instead of a harmful, knee-jerk reaction.

Success Actions That Work: People will not always (or even usually) act the way you expect them to. Understanding this will make you a more effective manager. You can't change it, but you *can* change your response.

Experiment with the techniques above to see which ones best put you back in control. You may find that one technique works best in the moment of conflict and quickly gets you back in control of the situation while another helps you get to a better place over time so that things do not ruffle your feathers as easily as they used to. New research in this area continues to be released at an amazing speed so check out Bestsuccessfactors.com for additional suggestions.

When you learn to stay calm even in the most stressful situation, you will gain respect from others. Your relationships will change for the better, and you will be more appreciated. And of course, you will increase your chances of getting that promotion you are seeking.

Question: My friends say I'm a born cynic. But only fools believe everything they're told. My mantra: "I doubt that. Prove it." I think there's a big difference between being negative (bad) and having a healthy dose of skepticism (good). Does the research support me on this? Or do I need to somehow recast myself into an optimist to be highly successful?

Cynicism in tiny doses doesn't have to be an evil filter. In fact, without a few healthy doses of cynicism the bad guys would run over the good guys and the world would not be a better place. Being on guard is useful when it comes to protecting your livelihood and your family.

Plenty of people are not well intentioned and do not have your best interests at heart. The reality is that there are those who want to see harm come to you and your business and they will take action to prevent you from achieving.

Research by Dr. Martin Seligman, the world's preeminent researcher on optimism, has found that optimistic people have a significantly less realistic view of life than do pessimists. A healthy dose of cynicism can help you see real danger. It is often helpful in just about everything from making your business grow to traveling the world and choosing a safe hotel to stay at. A healthy dose of cynicism is like castor oil. It can taste nasty, but it can help you live longer and achieve more.

But, overdo cynicism and pessimism and you run into some big problems. If you are so cynical that you doubt your potential competence and ability to get things done, you need to change your outlook.

Pessimists have three tendencies that crush their ability to achieve:

1. They make failure their fault. It becomes all about them. They personalize all negative results.
2. They see failure as something that will happen over and over again.
3. They view failure as something that will happen across a broad spectrum of life instead of just one area.

In its extreme, pessimism can move from doubt about others (their ability, dedication, or likelihood to achieve, in our case) to a jaded negativity about their intent. And then you have a mess. In pessimism, you have failure that breeds failure and a person that is permanently held hostage by his beliefs. Escape becomes highly unlikely for most that are stuck in pessimism's grasp.

Success Actions That Work: Do you need to reform yourself into an optimist to succeed? No, you don't. Particularly if this means putting your trust in the wrong people or adopting wishful thinking.

"It would hurt that man's feelings if I didn't get into the elevator with him."

"The lottery will strike here."

"Just believe and it will happen."

"Expect a miracle."

You will not hear this type of optimism come from a top achiever's mouth. A highly successful person would not even consider it. Why? Because these types of statements cede control to another power.

When you are out of control and putting your life, your relationship, your business, or your income into someone else's hands without a healthy dose of cynicism, you are acting foolishly and neglecting your responsibility. Errant optimism and wishful thinking weaken your control.

Take a hard look in the mirror and see if you are operating with a healthy dose of cynicism or whether you are sabotaging yourself by personalizing failure and repeating the same types of mistakes. The real judge of whether your outlook is working for you is whether you get things done and are showing rapid progress over time. If cynicism is impeding your progress, you must change it. Now.

If you are operating with a healthy level of skepticism and your outlook is working for you, then keep on doing what you are doing.

Question: **My life in a nutshell: So much to do, so little time. I am constantly overwhelmed by the demands in my life. How do I start regaining control and feel more confident?**

It sounds like you are feeling overwhelmed by the vast number of things that you need to do. It does not matter if we are talking about work or your personal life. Too much on your plate leaves you in a constant state of being overwhelmed. This ends up pushing your buttons and causing nothing to be achieved as it should be.

You feel overwhelmed because your body cannot take in and process all of the information that is required of it. More so, you are in a constant state of overload in every activity that you do, which just intensifies the worry, frustration, and the lack of concentration that you have. Research shows that feeling so overwhelmed that you feel like you just cannot complete a task is a common cause of procrastination.

Let's say that you have a large and important project on your desk. There are many steps to accomplishing it, and it will take time to go through the project, organize, and accomplish it. You instantly feel overwhelmed. You can feel it in your shoulders, in your head and all of a sudden, you just can no longer focus on the process. Perhaps you are not sure where you should start the project. You may even feel as if the task is so large or so hard that you do not have the skills or the ability to complete it or complete all of it. Perhaps you do not think you have all of the information and tools to get the job done right. Instead of accomplishing the task, then, you put it off to the side for another day.

This type of procrastination happens because you'd rather tackle something that you know you can handle. That big project just feels too difficult. Whether you intend to go back and complete the project or not, you have now sidestepped the job so that you can gain the comfort and the benefit of completing a task that is easier for you to do. Ahhhh. Instant gratification.

Because the job you set aside was important, you realize at the last minute that you need to complete it, and the overwhelming worry starts up all over again. Except now your problem is magnified. Time is now so limited that you are less able to focus and less able to complete the job with the same quality that you could have done beforehand, despite your doubts.

Important jobs and projects that are larger and harder do not just go away. They cannot be shoved under the carpet until the next day, week, or whenever you get to it. If you do that, you are not likely to be able to complete the project as well as you could complete it if you did it today, with your full attention, and enough time to do it right.

Time. There just is not enough of it. That is the first thing that you need to face. There is not enough time in the day to do all of the things that you want to.

You have to make decisions, and smart ones, about what can be done, what should be done, and what there simply is not enough time to do. Translate that as some people and some tasks have to get the axe. Yes, that is a bummer. It also is 100 percent necessary if you are going to live without hypertension for the rest of your life.

In order to avoid being overwhelmed, you need to learn how to maximize use of every hour of the day. This means using each hour of your day to do the right things to accomplish all of the tasks that you need to in the most efficient manner.

Your goal should be to always work on the most important parts of your tasks. When you focus on only what is important, you can transform the way that you think and relieve a lot of the stresses that you face. Focus on the most important aspects of your day, and you will always make the very best use of your time.

Success Actions That Work: Here are five simple things to do right now to get started on the right track.

1. Make the decision that you cannot accomplish everything that you want all at one time. You need patience to move from a state of being overwhelmed to being a successful time manager.

2. Relax your mind. You need to be able to focus on what you need to do and how to accomplish it. When you can relax your mind from its frantic, overwhelmed state, you are better able to see what is the most important aspect of your task. Build regular 10- to 15-minute time-outs into your daily schedule.

3. Set priorities with a long-term focus. When it comes to deciding what is the most important thing to accomplish at this moment, go with what will have the best long-term implications. When you read the chapter on wealth building, you will find that a key to building wealth is to do activities now that pay in the future. Keep your eye on the long run. If you work only for today, you're more likely to stay in bed.

4. Write it down. People who are successful at planning their time have a list of projects and daily activities that they need to tackle. This way, you can see what is in front of you, make decisions about their importance, and not feel like there is no end in sight. Include everything you can on the list that you need to accomplish, small and big. Then, invest the time in organizing your list from the most important to the least important. If you don't know exactly what needs to get done today, you are going to forget to do things. Sometimes even important things. As you get something done, cross it off your list. (Of course, do not put a line through anything that you work on that does not get done. Finish the job.)

5. Get a planner and plan your day. Plan out what you need to accomplish in blocks of time. Planners are structured by the hour but high achievers get things done by the project. People who live by the hour do not make as much money as people who live by the project. Block your time to get complete projects or pieces of projects done.

These five things are simple, right? You can begin to accomplish them right now in a matter of minutes. When you schedule your time to accomplish your goals and your tasks, your mind will be less overwhelmed and you will be more likely to achieve your goals. These simple steps will help you overcome the overwhelmed feeling you have. Do this and see what your results are. You may find yourself in the best position that you have been in for a long time. Once you are in a better place, you will be ready to incorporate additional tools for success.

9

Resilience

Resilience is related to perseverance. Both are needed for success. As talked about in Chapter 1, perseverance is an essential part of self-discipline. To persevere means to refuse to stop. It means to maintain a state of unbending and unyielding movement toward an outcome. You keep on going no matter what.

Resilience is a broader concept and means that you are doing the things you need to do to give yourself the ability to bounce back from setbacks. Resilience includes fueling yourself mentally, physically, emotionally, and spiritually so that you have the ability to keep going after failure, illness, death of a loved one, and other crises. All of these things happen along the road to success. Only people who bounce back from them will succeed in the long run.

Resilience is about proactively recognizing that there will be ups and downs on the path to success and learning how to use both the good and hard days to keep going and growing. It requires that you give sincere thought to what is most important to you in your life and make decisions to give time to these things. It also requires that you make smart decisions on a daily basis to refill your energy reservoirs.

A shining example of what resilience looks like is Lance Armstrong. He made history by winning the Tour de France, the most demanding bicycle race in the world, seven times in a row.

He also is known for his extraordinary battle against and victory over testicular cancer. His ability to beat the odds against this aggressive form of cancer represents a greater victory than his repeated Tour de France championships. Far beyond his accomplishments on a bike, Armstrong has become a champion for cancer patients, giving them new hope to fight their own battles and lobbying for cancer research funding.

When you read Armstrong's memoir, *It's Not About the Bike* (Armstrong 2000), you come to appreciate how he viewed both his athletic training and his fight against cancer as a personal journey that presented a wide variety of challenges for body, mind, and spirit. It was a journey that was *continuous* with growth, discoveries, learning, setbacks, and new beginnings.

When you learn the art of resilience, it becomes clear that your journey to success really has no final destination. You cross some finish lines along the way, but only on your way to the next challenge. You see that the purpose of moving down the path that you are on becomes one of continual transformation, growth, and renewal. As you progress in your journey, the definition of what you see as possible also gets bigger and bigger.

An important part of taking a major setback and turning it into a comeback is to give meaning to your struggles and make sense of them within the journey of your own life. In an interview after winning his final Tour de France, Armstrong went so far as to say that he didn't think that he would have won a single Tour had he not experienced such an advanced and aggressive type of cancer. He actually gave his cancer and his experiences overcoming it the *credit* for his Tour victories. He gave meaning to his struggles and used that meaning to fuel subsequent successes.

When you walk the path to success, you will experience set-backs. You will experience a range of emotions as you respond to demanding situations. You will experience the physical demands of business training and competition. Success and personal develop-ment bring joys and hardships, progress and setbacks, successes and failures. Resilience helps you handle the ups, the downs, and all of the hills and valleys in between. You learn to handle adversity, take risks, learn from mistakes, and move on to the next level.

Mastering the skills we have already talked about, including self-discipline, perseverance, commitment, responsibility, belief, courage, confidence, and positive mental attitude, will help fuel resilience. Resilience also includes "softer" characteristics such as self knowledge, inner strength, patience, humility, flexibility, and a sense of enjoyment and fun.

Having fun is often overlooked as a component of success. When you look at successful people, you see that they achieve success by doing something that they are good at *and* something they love. When you look at the lives of people who live unfulfilling and less successful lives, you see that while they often have as much skill as those who are more successful in their field, they are not doing work that they love.

True success has components of joy and excitement for doing what you do on a daily basis. Successful people harbor a love for the process. As soft as this may sound, a high-achieving and truly competitive spirit allows you to open up to your greatest potential while enjoying the process of personal growth.

All three of us authors have our own version of a dream list or a "get to do" list. These lists have provided inspiration and direction in our lives. They provide an anchor when we feel life's winds blow strong against us. If you have not already done this, sit down right now and begin one for yourself. Create a list of things that you want to accomplish. Write down your dreams, your desires, your must haves, your must not haves, and who you want to take on your journey with you. Over time, you will add to the list. You also might take a few things off the list as you progress through life.

Once you have written your list of things you want to do or accomplish, get to work prioritizing them and taking action. Something amazing happens at this point. The minute you write down your dreams and take small actions toward achieving them, your brain will go to work pointing out connections and opportunities that have been around you the whole time. This is not mystical mumbo jumbo. It is your brain's reticular activating system at work. We have all had the experience of buying something that we thought was unique, only to notice that once we have bought it we see it everywhere.

Your brain is scanning your environment all the time. When it sees an activity or a thing like the one you are taking action on, it will let you know. You can then choose to act or not. It is up to you. But you will have the awareness and the opportunity.

Here is the real trick of high achievers, though. As soon as you see the opportunity, do not wait. Seize the moment. Do it. Reward yourself for your observation. There is no better time than right now to start achieving whatever your goal is. And oftentimes the only thing stopping you . . . is you.

Spend your life doing something that you enjoy. Continually learn more about it, get better every day, put out high-quality material or products, take excellent care of your clients, and have fun along the way. Many successes are born this way. When you are following your dreams and doing whatever it is you love, you will naturally build up your resiliency to help get you through whatever challenges come your way.

Here is what we want you to do right now. Yes, before you read the next paragraph. Lay down this book and take action on one thing you have already learned. We are serious. Stop reading right now and *do something* that will move you forward. The rest of the words will be here when you get back.

Question: **Is there really such a thing as life balance? If there is, I haven't found it. What are the magic keys?**

Many people have bought into the concept of a balanced life. As consultants and coaches, we often hear people say that they want to be "successful" and live a "balanced life."

The conversation usually goes something like this.

"What is a balanced life to you?"

"I want to be successful in my career but still have time each day for my family, friends, leisure, and relaxation."

"Do you like your current job?"

"No, I don't. I'm just putting in my time, you know? But it pays the bills. Maybe you have some ideas . . . on how to make it better?"

This type of life balance is an illusion. It makes a good picture in a movie. But it is a recipe for a disastrous plan in most peoples' lives.

The core problem is that there are very few jobs that provide enough income to offset future financial hardship in someone's life. In other words, when someone in the family becomes disabled, divorced, sick, dies, or gets fired (downsized, sorry) everything gets exponentially worse. Credit becomes stretched and then extinguished. All of these things devastate families and remove achievement and success from the picture. Survival becomes the issue.

So, in the present, the breadwinners settle for lives of working at jobs they hate and then going home and vegging out to make up for their miserable days. Then, one day, they must quit their jobs or be forced out when a disaster hits. They do not have savings stored up for the "rainy day" (which usually lasts several months and often the rest of the person's life). The rainy day requires replacing lost income as well as covering the additional enormous expenses that go with the rainy day, such as hospital bills or rebuilding the house that burned down.

Because someone had a leisurely nonworking life, they didn't have further education to prepare them for their next career. This education is necessary in the twenty-first century because most nonservice, nonsales jobs are being outsourced. Companies are hiring cheaper, highly educated Asians to replace modestly educated Americans. So the rainy day hits and the person can't get a new job that pays what the old one did. The entire family suffers and usually for years.

What was seemingly an okay trade-off (putting up with the job you hate for the leisure time you crave) is actually a short-term illusion. When disaster hits, neither parent (if there are two parents) is able to stay home with the child that needs help because they will now be working two jobs to replace the one better paying job they had. The parents may be able to replace their income if they are still together but they will rarely see their children or watch a TV show again.

How many people does this happen to? A lot. In other words, it very well could happen to you.

How do you know if you are safe?

You really do not know with certainty but you have a margin of error if your liquid assets (your savings not including retirement or your home equity) minus your credit card and vehicle debt are greater than one-half year's worth of living expenses. You need a minimum cushion of liquid assets that is equal to six months of your current living expenses.

This is why we strongly recommend that people start or buy a small business, preferably one they love. Do something that is fun or rich with meaning. Most small businesses cost next to nothing to start and can create an income much higher than working for someone else. This business also will help increase the portion of expenses that are tax deductible (home, business, and education that will pay off shortly after the expense is incurred).

So, does any of this apply to you if you love your job? If someone loves his job, he is in a potentially good life situation. Work that is meaningful and secured by an individual's strong skills that make him almost irreplaceable is a nice beginning. Of course, that still only looks at today. The other piece is saving enough money for that rainy day in the future.

Success Actions That Work: We stay away from life balance with our clients and work more on life integration and focus. Life doesn't need to be balanced if it is seamless and focused.

A focused life is one where the breadwinners love what they do today and can take care of the rainy day in the future. They know that life is short—sometimes unfairly so. They take care of their family today and have a monetary cushion for the rainy day. Additionally they have their retirement taken care of.

Do you really want to live a life where you have to offset something bad with something good? The person who strives for balancing bad and good is unlikely to do well at any level and lives with an insecure future. We challenge you to name 10 people who are successful in your field and had balanced lives on their journeys to success. If you hate part of your life, change it. Then all parts of your life will become better.

The integrated and focused life is self-balancing because all day you are engaged in meaningful, important, fun, and interesting activity that is taking care of you and your family today and into the future. You are living the life of *your* choosing. This can include working at your own business or at a job you love and find important.

A focused life is the only type of life that brings families stability, security, safety, and long-term happiness. People who live a focused life almost always win and have a fulfilling and meaningful life. Focused lives, like balanced lives, will have their disasters and crises. But a person whose life is focused will weather these setbacks more easily. Move from attempting to live a balanced life to creating an integrated and focused life, and you will be moving toward a higher level of achievement.

Question: My life was really going well. I probably didn't appreciate how well. But then a few big things happened—relationships, finances—that put me in a tailspin. I feel like that TV ad, "Help! I've fallen and I can't get up." How do I start rebuilding?

Bad things happen to good people. It's a fact of life. One of the most extraordinary things about human beings is our capacity for resilience in the face of setbacks and trauma.

Miraculous survival and recovery are not occasional happenings in the world. Every day, someone survives a tragedy. Every day, someone takes another step toward a happier life despite a past trauma. Every day, life goes on, and we adjust. And we are stronger for it.

You may need professional care to get back up. The suggestions made here are obviously not substitutes for such care. However, many people have found the following strategies effective for relieving the stress of trauma and taking back control of their lives. Whether you choose to seek professional help or embark on a healing path yourself, know that you can break free and begin to live again after tragedy touches you. You do not have to let trauma keep you from achieving what you want out of life.

1. Normalize

When small disasters strike (the audit letter arrives, the power goes out, you have a little fender bender), remind yourself that these are experiences shared by many of your fellow humans.

Life is not easy and it is not fair. All of the emotions you are feeling are simply a part of being human. You are not being picked on or victimized. Don't take it personally. It can help to remember that others are feeling your pain.

2. Find the Humor

For small setbacks, sometimes laughter really is the best medicine. If you are able to look at the situation objectively, you may be able to laugh at it, or at least realize that it could have been much worse.

Try to imagine what your situation would look like in a TV sitcom. Simply use your imagination and imagine all the ways in which the setback or trauma could have been worse. Let's say you bounced a check, ended up having to pay a fee to the bank and had to postpone paying one of your bills or go without something you planned to purchase. Now, imagine what might have happened if you bounced multiple checks. You might have had to put off several payments. The snowball effect could have caused you to lose your car or have your power shut off. Your bills could have spiraled out of control, eventually leaving you standing on the corner homeless. Can you see this situation play out on *Seinfield*? It could be funny watching it as a comedy.

Obviously this isn't going to work for every situation. Actually losing your home or car qualifies as major trauma, for which dramatization is not always effective. But for some people at some times, humor sure can help put things in perspective.

3. Remind Yourself of the Resilient Human Spirit

Another approach is to research actual cases to find similar situations that other people have endured that turned out worse than yours. No, the idea is not to see how lucky you were. It is to remind you of human resiliency: *your ability to survive.*

You can search online for news stories or browse the periodicals archive at your local library. Generally, you will always be able to find cases concerning people who had more difficulty than you, yet survived. You will too. After all, you're still alive.

4. Give Meaning to Your Experiences

Another approach many find helpful is to write about their experiences. The simple act of getting the experience out of your head and on to paper can help you feel better. Research shows that writing about details of what happened and how you felt about the events leads your mind to start generating solutions about what steps to take next. Journaling can help you make sense of your experiences and see how they fit into the bigger picture of your life.

If you are ready to take an additional step (this takes courage and you will need to dig deep), do something to help others in your situation. Make a donation to a specific person or situation or a related charity. Or start a support program or fund-raising drive in your community. Taking action, no matter how small, often helps to alleviate the feelings of loss and helplessness associated with traumatic experiences. It also can help you give meaning to your losses.

Success Actions That Work: You can choose just one or any combination of the above techniques to work on rebuilding your life. If you are uncomfortable with an approach or it is not working for you, move on to another one.

Welcome to the human experience. You might be down right now but that doesn't mean you need to stay down. If possible, find something to laugh about. Imagining how much worse things could have been, can put setbacks in perspective and help you feel better. Reminding yourself of how others survived and thrived in a similar situation also can help reduce stress and put you in a better place to cope with your challenges. And using your experiences to help others not only gets your mind off of your own problems, but it can help heal your wounds.

We hope that you find one of these techniques helpful as you work through your current situation. With time and action, you may even come to see that your setbacks can provide the seeds for additional growth.

Question: **I manage a great team, but some of them are burning the candle at both ends and it's starting to affect their performance and team morale. I don't want these key employees to burn out or quit on me. What specific things can I do to help them get stronger or work smarter?**

As a manager, you understand the pressures in today's business world. You are not alone in finding it difficult to support valuable team members and protect them from mental, physical, and emotional burnout. It's no wonder that burnout is a concern, given the increasing demands to deliver more with less time and fewer resources.

You have a front-row seat to watch your team face conflicting demands, long working hours, and constant change in a tough and quickly changing business environment. Especially in this time of more frequent layoffs, good employees find themselves absorbing more work, spending longer hours at the office and less time at home, and forgoing the type of self-care that is needed for a continuous level of high performance.

It sounds like your team members are passionate about what they do, so that's not the problem. They have the "why" in place and that is important. Work is simply becoming less fun and enjoyable for them because they are using up all of their mental, physical, and emotional reserves.

You want to make sure that your team sees you as being on their side. An effective manager is an ally and a resource for employees to help handle challenges and pressure, not the enemy. One of the best ways to be seen this way is by regularly communicating face to face with team members in a relaxed and confidential manner. Encourage your staff to talk about their challenges and then partner with them to find resources and strategies to meet these challenges.

As a manager, you need to have your finger on the pulse of your team and frequently check in to see how they are doing. It is common for people to deal with pressure by bottling it up inside. Research shows that this can lead to increased stress, high blood pressure, low self-confidence, and other health problems. All of these things reduce a person's productivity, ability to focus, and job satisfaction.

If you don't give your staff opportunities to talk about their challenges, this negative, bottled up energy will begin to leak out and affect others in the office. Your employees may begin feeling sorry for themselves, complaining to each other, or even emotionally exploding. Obviously these types of nonproductive behaviors would negatively affect both individual and team productivity.

A general lack of physical activity, combined with increased physical tension and stress, can further undermine your team's ability to effectively handle the demands of a competitive business world. Resiliency requires smart decision making on a daily basis. No one can sit for hours in front of a computer, on the phone, or in meetings and sustain a high level of energy and stamina. Without regular and proper breaks, one's body slowly becomes drained of energy. Maintaining a sedentary work life results in fatigue, poor concentration, disinterest, and a lower level of performance.

It sounds as if some of your employees need to be educated about taking regular minibreaks in order to optimize their performance. Your hard-working employees might think that they will get more done if they eat lunch at their desks while reading documents, answering e-mails, and returning calls, but this type of behavior cannot be sustained over time. Repeated stress without sufficient rest will lead to a lack of engagement and burnout. Encourage your staff to get up and move around after completing a task. Simply taking their eyes off the computer screen and stretching for a few minutes will help them feel better and perform better.

So, what can you do as a manager? Here are a few ideas to help keep your team on a high-performance track and buffer them from burnout.

1. Regularly Check In

In a high-pressured office, it is easy for employees to get on that old hamster wheel and fall into a rut, get overwhelmed, or feel unappreciated. Without establishing regular ways to talk about how they are doing, you may not know how far an employee has been pushed until the day he walks into your office to say he is quitting.

Schedule a regular, brief check-in time to connect with each key team member. Depending on the staff position, this might be weekly or even daily. Ask open-ended questions that allow your employees to talk about how they are feeling. Specifically ask about what support they feel they need to accomplish their tasks.

This isn't the time for you to add to the pressure they are under so limit your feedback to the issues your employees raise. It is important to keep these sessions short so you don't increase the time pressures your team members are feeling. To help keep these check-ins brief, you might want to call them "stand up" meetings.

These check-in sessions will help you to keep your finger on your team's pulse and create opportunities for social connection and problem solving. More importantly, they will reduce your employees' stress levels by giving them a chance to voice their questions and concerns. As you help your stressed out employees feel that they have been heard and understood, it is likely that they also will become better listeners, which will benefit your whole team.

2. Build in Minibreaks to Refuel and Refocus

As a manager, you need to help your staff physically break up their day with movement. Incorporate activity into your staff's day. Create a culture that encourages employees to get away from their desk during lunch and for mid morning and afternoon breaks.

We all need to take time out during the day to recharge our batteries. When working with individuals, we generally teach them how to work in a very intense and very focused manner for 60 to 90 minutes. During this time, you don't leave whatever you are working on. You committed to get the project done. Do it. Then take a break. Close your eyes and empty your mind. Go outside and get some fresh air. Go walk a mile. Meditate. Do what you need to do to refresh and refuel. Then on to your next project.

Get creative incorporating activity and short breaks into your staff's day. Encourage them to take the stairs or go outside for a few minutes of fresh air. Or you can conduct your regular check-ins during brief morning or afternoon "walk and talk" sessions where you take a short walk to discuss any pressing challenges and issues.

If your staff members are resistant to the idea of taking mini refueling breaks or need reminders to form better habits, you can install stretching software on their computer that will regularly prompt them to stand up, stretch, or take a quick break. Or you can assign tasks to these staff members that get them away from their desks. For instance, ask them to run out and pick up the lunch. Then sit down and eat together while everyone uses the time to connect, laugh, and refuel.

3. Give Permission to Leave Work at the Office

Deadlines loom and projects need to get done. And sometimes this requires additional hours at the office. That's part of achieving at a high level. But continually working long hours without a clean break from the work environment can lead to burnout. Your staff will undermine their health and the long-term success of your team if they don't understand the need to use time away from the office to completely *switch off* the work mode.

We all need our minds and bodies to switch off at night and get sufficient, high quality sleep to heal, regenerate and repair. When pushed and pushed to stay in work mode for long periods of time, the body loses the ability to wind down and relax. Sleep becomes interrupted and restless and can lead to a sleep disorder. Without sufficient deep sleep, one's body cannot sustain a high level of motivation and productivity.

Identify those members of your team who are at high risk of burnout. You know what to look for. Do you have staff members who take pride in how much face time they put in at the office? Have they developed habits like regularly working extra long hours, being available on their mobile phone at any time, and answering e-mails from home? Do they look tired and you hear complaints that they didn't sleep well because they had so much on their minds? Have they begun to interact with other team members in a negative way? Is the quality of their work declining or have they stopped enjoying the work they do??

Talk with your high-risk employees and help hem to identify the tradeoffs they are making to put in so many work hours. Find out what relationships might need to be nourished and then arrange a fun night out for them to do this. Find out what hobbies and interests they have given up in order to put in the longer hours at work and then sponsor a related activity. What would they love to do if only they "had the time"? Support them in taking the time to pursue this passion.

Good managers create a culture of leaving work at work. Encourage your team to use vacation time. Consider a "use it or lose it" policy if needed to promote regular breaks from the office. Suggest that employees take a personal day or "mental health day" when you see they need the break. Remember to lead by example and limit your off-hours work interactions with your team.

Success actions that work: Some managers might count themselves fortunate, in the short term, if they had a team that was all about work. You are wise to see that no one can sustain a high level of productivity over time if they don't regularly take breaks and work smart.

You mentioned that members of your team are burning the candle at both ends. We suspect that they are spending long hours at the office without a clean break away. It might be that even when their bodies are away, their minds continue to ruminate about work issues. To prevent burnout in your team, create a culture of open communication, productivity and efficiency. Allow and encourage your employees to switch off the work mode.

If burnout becomes a widespread issue for your team, take it seriously and get outside resources to educate them on the importance of relaxing and unwinding. Bring in an instructor to teach meditation, yoga, stretching, or pilates. Begin offering regular in-office chair massages. Sponsor memberships to a nearby gym and create incentives to use them or schedule regular workout times. If appropriate, you may want to offer flextime, where staff members can start early and finish early or start late and finish late, or allow them to do some work from home.

The dangers of pending burnout, both for your employees' sake and for the overall morale and productivity of your team, are real. Take the initiative to help your team refuel, reengage, and bring the fun back into your team's daily work life. Doing this will keep your employees energized, enthusiastic, and motivated to come to work and give their best efforts.

10
Wealth Building

Success is achieving whatever it is that you've set out to do in your life. It is the mental state that allows you to accomplish your goals and live your life to your fullest ability and capacity. The definition of success is purely individual and measured by you. Your definition of success may or may not include the accumulation of money and things. Yet, for most people, the definition of success is or includes financial freedom. Financial freedom simply means that you can live on what you have today for the rest of your life if you chose to.

How important is wealth building to you? What is your definition of "wealthy" or "rich?" What kind of lifestyle do you want to live? One of the most important things that you can do when deciding on a goal or starting down a path is to clearly define what success looks like so you know when to quit. Far too often people keep going long after they've reached the goal because they didn't know what completion looked like. They just kept putting out the effort without looking at the result. You can't complete any task for which you don't have a definition of the finished product.

We include wealth building as a core aspect of achievement because money is a key tool of success. It provides security so you can focus on other things. It provides freedom. It allows you to live your life to the fullest. And it buys you opportunities to create additional success.

Wealth is not wired into anyone's genes. Your unconscious motives actually move you toward comfort and away from building wealth. *And unconscious motives are very powerful drivers of most behavior*. It takes great effort for conscious thought to become an even more powerful driver of behavior.

For example, the vast majority of people predisposed to being overweight and obese will stay that way because their unconscious motives are greater than conscious thought. As anyone who's lost 500 pounds (over the years) will tell you, it is tough to overcome the unconscious mind. You can go all day being good and then pig out before bedtime, undoing an entire day's worth of willpower.

To override the unconscious mind, you cannot let your guard down until you have altered your dominant drives. It is that simple. The unconscious drives are so strong that it takes a planned, determined and driven desire at the conscious level to overcome your unconscious feelings and emotions. Once the drives are altered, then they become drivers toward the desired behaviors.

People simply are not unconsciously predisposed to wealth.

People are predisposed to consume . . . now.

To eat now.

To drink now.

To feel good now.

To want to be calm now.

To want to be out of pain now.

To want to be secure now.

To want to relax and be comfortable now.

There is very little genetic predisposition toward anything that would lead you to wealth.

There is no "save for a rainy day" gene.

There is no "men be a responsible dad" gene.

There is no "money consciousness" gene.

Wealth building is about conscious decisions overcoming hard-wired programming, programming that only a small percentage of people ever conquer.

Fortunately, the opportunity to be among these elite achievers is available to most people in most free countries. You are born with the right to pursue wealth and the potential to be rich. Your income is largely self-determined. There are always unexpected variables, but the fact is, it is your choice as to what you want to earn and you will likely earn what you want to earn. You will decide what is enough and what is not. If you are willing to forgo some things in life (read as trade-offs) and are very focused, you can work on building as big a bank account as you want.

Wealth begins with a mind-set. It is what you choose to think and act upon that produces the wealth you want. When you stop acting to produce wealth then you stop building wealth. What you think will be ... pretty much will be.

Research shows that wealthy people tend to get wealthy using similar thinking processes (and so do poor people). To create wealth, you need to think like a wealthy person and then put your thinking into action. It comes down to a very specific wealth building mind-set.

The mind-set of many people is to be preoccupied with a job as an employee. They forget or unintentionally fail to cross the line at some point in life to see how they can create real wealth. Just like a coin, there are two sides to earning money and many people never bother to find out what it looks like on the other side.

Example: Who is on the face of a $100 bill? Of course. Ben Franklin.

Now, what's on the back of the $100 bill?

Exactly. You don't carry hundreds?

Okay.

Who's on the front of the $5 bill?

Of course, it's Abraham Lincoln.

And what's on the back?

The Lincoln Memorial.

Few people know this without looking.

Reality point: Change is the generator of wealth.

If you are not wealthy and you want to become wealthy, you need to become someone you are not. In order to get different results, you are going to have to take different actions. You are going to need to be different. You are going to need to make changes inside and out. You do not have to change everything about yourself, but you do have some heavy tweaking to do.

Many people will say, "I am who I am, and I'm not changing one bit for anything or anyone." Good luck. Change is a requirement for success. You may currently feel that you do not want to change. Do not be scared by this concept. It is not your personality or your character that need renovation. It is your daily habits, actions, focus, projects, judgment, and decisions. To get different results, you have to change things.

Now, back to the $100 bill. The back has a nice engraving of Independence Hall. People are so used to viewing life through one very specific lens that they fail to see entire pictures. The problem is, when it comes to wealth, you really want to know what is on the reverse side of that $100 bill.

It is an interesting coincidence that Independence Hall is on the back of the $100 bill, the largest note used in circulation in the United States.

Independence . . . being wealthy. See the connection?

Question: **Can you get wealthy as a long-term employee or do you need to become an entrepreneur? I am in my early 40s. I like my job and entrepreneurship doesn't appeal to me, but I want to make sure that I will be able to retire securely.**

Wealth begins with a mind-set. If you set your mind to work for somebody else, you will get a job and you will become comfortable and familiar working as an employee. If you set your mind to attaining a higher level of financial freedom, you may decide to assume more risk and find the means of becoming wealthy without the challenges of working for someone else.

The reality is that the person at risk is most likely to have wealth. Employers provide jobs and that is a gift. When someone gives you a job, that person is taking a 100 percent risk on you and you take zero risk in return. That is a gift.

When you go into business, you eventually become an employer yourself. You take your money and give it to someone else in exchange for someone performing some set of duties or projects. If people don't understand that the person writing the check is the person who is at risk, they will have difficulty building their own wealth.

It is a fascinating paradox that being at risk is the surest way to build wealth.

Now, there is nothing wrong with having a job and working for someone else. It sounds like you enjoy your work. And it can be less stressful to have someone else provide direction over what set of tasks you need to do each day. But jobs do not provide a high level of financial security because they don't have renewable resources (sales, renewals.) And they rarely provide wealth.

We challenge you to use your job as a place where you get paid to learn about business. Very few people can simply graduate from high school or college and immediately begin to build wealth with their own business. Schools can teach you some but not all of what you will need to know to be successful in a business of your own. If you do decide to start your own business and put yourself at risk, you'll need knowledge of areas like marketing, advertising, sales, accounting and taxes, administration, product development, product research, and investment. Mastering these skills is beyond the scope of traditional education (even if you take classes that have those names attached to them.) These are skills that turn risk into calculated risk. Good risk.

For those with aspirations to run their own businesses, the best way to prepare is to get your feet wet in as many aspects of a company as you can. By watching how the people who have money at risk in a company make decisions, you see what it takes to succeed or fail. You get to see what works and what doesn't, up close and personal, for free.

Watching a CEO is interesting and it might provide useful connections, but you also want to study those who work in marketing, advertising, and sales. Salespeople are revenue generators, not just employees. Without them the company dies. And a lot of salespeople in many different companies have become wealthy, very wealthy. How? Salespeople determine their own income.

Success Actions That Work: As long as you are in a job, learn while you earn. And while you're doing so, be a huge asset to your company. Make it so that when you leave your company, they will have a very hard time replacing you for the same money. The mind-set of people who are eventually going to move from employment to building wealth is to create as much success for their current employer as possible. Be loyal to your company, help a division grow, train an awesome sales team, and so forth. Then take those skills and knowledge into your own adventures.

So, is it impossible to create wealth as an employee? Of course not. If you make an unusually valuable contribution to your company and are paid extremely well, you may be able to create financial security . . . over a long period of time. You will need to spend much less than you earn, save the difference, and let compound interest work for you. This takes self-discipline and a lot of time.

If you want to stay with your company, explore opportunities for increasing your value to the company and, if appropriate, assuming more risk. Sam Walton and Bill Gates created a lot of millionaires who were willing to work for stock and cash instead of just cash. Those people gambled on their companies' business plans, and won big. Again, there was risk involved.

The reality is that most people in a corporation outside of sales and upper management (and this does not provide an automatic pass to wealth) will not become wealthy from their jobs. Unless your job provides you with the opportunity to earn more by assuming a higher level of risk or responsibility, you should give careful consideration to running your own small business on the side.

We repeatedly have seen (and experienced) that the most direct path to wealth is to run a successful business of your own. Every person who works for someone else should seriously consider having a small business on the side. It can be either Internet-based or a brick and mortar operation, but it should be something where you determine your own income. For more guidance on this essential building block of financial freedom, go to Bestsuccessfactors.com. Take action on this essential wealth building strategy today.

Question: **Have researchers looked at how the rich actually make their money? Has anyone created a blueprint for wealth that actually works?**

The wealthy people of the world are some of the most studied and carefully analyzed people there are. The rich and famous represent a microscopic percentage of the overall population. The wealthy represent our dreams, our goals, and our aspirations.

As very young adults, many dream of being rich. When you were younger you probably felt that you would strike it rich early and would live an abundant life. As time passes by, you start to believe less and less that you are deserving of being wealthy. You look at those who got lucky and became rich and wonder how they were able to make it.

It had to be luck because they made it and you didn't and you worked hard.

One day you get lucky and have a chance to sit down with a couple of millionaires. After talking to them you wonder, "How the heck did they get so rich, because they are nothing special." Eventually you conclude that the wealthy are not necessarily brilliant, talented, skillful, or amazing after all. So, what happened?

The notion of "getting rich" has been the focus of countless books, tons of seminars, thousands of case studies, movies, stories, and examinations. The rich are carefully watched and studied and interviewed, yet many people are still left wondering "How did they even get so rich in the first place?"

Here is the secret: Becoming wealthy is a matter of choice. It is a matter of focus and a matter of taking consistent action toward your goals. Rich people got that way by following the same steps as everyone else who is, or ever has been, rich.

If being wealthy is something you want, then you need to find the footprints, and follow them. Success and wealth leave footprints. Those who succeed on this path leave clues. Become the Sherlock Holmes of finding success. Then follow the trail already blazed.

For example, research shows that there is one key decision your kids need to make to achieve and build wealth. The answers lie in the census and income numbers from the United States government. According to the 2006 census data, the median annual income for a family in the United States is $48,200. This means that half of the households earn more than this and the other half earn less.

How important is the education of the head of household to that family's income? Extremely important.

2006 Annual Household Income Averages (in thousands) by Education Level

Education	Median Household Income
No diploma	22.4
High school graduate	36.8
College graduate	68.7
Professional Degree	100.00

These figures suggest that when you get your kids to graduate from college, they will make nearly twice as much money as their non-college-graduate friends. The effect of a professional degree will help them earn nearly three times as much. With as quickly as technology is changing the economic landscape, this advantage may lessen in the future. But for now, a college degree undeniably gives your kids a competitive edge.

Success action point: If you are a parent, send your kids to college.

So what about you? What do you need to do to create wealth?

Revelation: One of the best ways to become rich is to do what rich people do.

You either choose to affiliate with successful people who can show you that a door is the part of a wall that leads to the next room or you beat your head on the wall until it hits a handle and pushes open the door (we did some of that in our earlier days.) Find someone who is rich in your field and do what they do. Follow that person and study him and ask him questions. You will ultimately plow your own path, with your own unique style, but you will be following the basic formula for wealth.

If you decide not to shorten the learning curve by finding a mentor or coach, then your job is this: Find the footprints, analyze them, understand them, and follow them in a bold manner. Once you have the formula to wealth, it is up to you to implement it.

Nobody (and we really mean *nobody*) can do this for you. Only you can implement this wealth formula. There will not be anybody coming to your aid. The responsibility is on your shoulders and no one else's. It is all up to you. Why? Because, you see, the footprints are there waiting for you to follow them and only you can walk for yourself. Nobody is going to carry you to the finish line. You have to walk for yourself.

We are all born with certain advantages and limitations. We differ in intelligence, disposition, emotional stability, strength, and attractiveness. You may be tall or short, healthy or ill, good looking or less attractive, young or old, black or white, a college graduate or a dropout, or anything else. Yes, some of these factors can make the path to wealth more challenging. But none of them make it impossible. If you are breathing and alive and can shovel snow, cut the lawn, use your mind, or telemarket, you can become wealthy. It does not matter how you were raised or who your parents were. It does not matter if you have been poor your entire life. None of that can completely shut the door to wealth.

If you can follow the wealth formula consistently, you can become wealthy. It will require that you make a solid and long-term commitment to becoming rich. It will require you to continue following this formula over time. (This doesn't mean that it will take a long time to become rich—that is up to you.)

It does not matter what industry you choose to pursue (as long as there is a willingness to pay and a demand for your product or service), building wealth is the same in almost every field. The rules are the same. The footprints are the same. You just need to know what they are and follow them.

Let's say that you determine that one part of your wealth formula is to work more hours on tasks that will continue to make you money in the future. You figure out how to give more effort to highly leveragable activities and you decide to do this by running an Internet business on the side. Each day, you begin work one hour earlier and end work one hour later. You use this time to complete important projects with big payoffs. By doing this, you will start to get results. And, you will become almost addicted to working hard and achieving results. You are creating momentum.

You will become someone who makes things happen and others will say to you, "You work too much." You're in good company with all people of achievement. If people did not say that to you in the past, and now they tell you that you work too hard, then guess what . . . you are changing and evolving. Commit to yourself right now that this is a very good thing indeed!

Many people who have become wealthy do not even realize what they have done to get that way. They just know that they have grown from where they used to be—when they were not wealthy.

Remember, to become wealthy you must be willing to evolve and change who you are. We are not talking about changing your morals, ethics, religion, or anything like that. (Well, actually, for some people, morals and ethics may need a gut check, but that's not what we are referring to when we talk about you changing your *self*.)

The simple fact is that if you are wealthy (unless you won the lottery or inherited your wealth), you did what other wealthy people did. If you are not, you did not. If you want to build wealth, you need to change some things about yourself and what you do. Here are eight tips to prepare you for these needed changes.

1. No one else will have more impact on your future from this point forward than you do.

You'll slowly sink or you'll learn to float, tread water, and swim. This decision and its follow-through are all charted and recorded in the brain. Your thoughts eventually affect your life. You choose your thoughts. You live with the results.

2. If you're broke, that doesn't mean you're out of the game.

Not by a long shot. The dollar amount in your debt column is not fixed. The income you have is not fixed. You decide what direction you're going to go over the next few years. Your journey will start with decisions that you reinforce daily to overcome natural drives. It takes work to overcome these biological drives. Not having money does not close off the path to wealth.

3. Take a break from your financial worries.

Instead of worrying about your financial problems, shift your focus to a different perspective. Take some time to relax and reenergize your brain so you can be more capable of finding the right solution. Set your problems aside for even just a few minutes each day, in order to allow your mind to come up with possible solutions.

4. Experience prosperity right now.

Take time each day to experience prosperity right where you now are in your life. Give yourself credit for earning every penny you have made. Look around at all you do have. When you accept that who you are is enough and what you have is enough for the moment, it puts you on more solid footing to move forward and create more.

5. Take failure as a chance to get smarter and stronger, by learning from it.

Don't ever let failure defeat you. Failure is a big part of the process of achievement. People who are afraid to lose or fail have little chance for achievement and wealth. Failing feels bad. It is frustrating. But what do most of your failures really mean? Not much. If the thought of failing is keeping you from going after what you want in life, you are taking yourself too seriously. Walk through the fear. Use failure to get tougher. Use failure to get smarter. Let it inspire and motivate you. When you do this and persevere, you will build wealth and success.

6. Control what you control.

We convince ourselves that it's easier to get others to change than to change ourselves. It is not. It's easier to *expect* others to change, but this is a dead-end street. You don't have control over others' attitudes. You control only yourself. Put your efforts toward developing self-control and all of the other components of achievement. This is what works to build wealth.

7. Be creative and open to new ideas.

Your mind is the single most powerful tool or asset you possess to gain financial security. Just like your body that takes nutrients from food and water, your mind must be continually energized with creative ideas and financial strategies to create and maintain wealth. Sometimes, we are so used to doing what the majority is doing that we completely close our minds to new ideas. People see the same things every day. They do the same things every day. Few people observe that Independence Hall is on the back of the $100 bill. The person who can create and implement will succeed.

8. Take calculated risks.

In the world of money, being smart is not enough. You've got to takes risks and action. You have to actualize or manifest what is in your mind. (This means going from thought to working model to final product.) Blatant risk taking without knowing how to make the calculations is dangerous and a recipe for financial disaster. Investing in thousands of dollars of inventory without having a plan in place to market and sell it is insane. Take smart and calculated risks.

Success Actions That Work: Here's a quick exercise for you: What is your annual income? Double this number and write it down on a piece of paper. Next, write down the date one year from today.

Now, if you were to write down everything you need to do to get to that higher annual income, you would have a list that would serve as the start of your action plan. As you write out this list, think about the changes you will need to make to reach the targeted income level.

Using this strategy would immediately set you apart from the 98 percent of the population that does not write down goals. By you doing so, you put yourself in the elite percentage of success-oriented people who set goals and make plans.

Getting more out of life requires doing more than the minimum. Get started today. Write down where you want to go and how you are going to get there. Then go to work on it. Leave no room to wonder if it can or will get done. You get it done. You are on your way to building greater wealth.

Question: **I'm reading a book about how to work only a few hours each week. How can I apply that to my sales job?**

The premise of a four-hour workweek is that you can outsource all of your work, leaving you a lifestyle that is free from worry and stress while your business goes on autopilot. It is an appealing concept. The hope is that you can work just a few hours per week and get rich.

Yet, part of what is wrong with many personal development books is that people make claims that aren't remotely accurate or true. But they do make great buzz for books.

Buzz is another way of saying "viral marketing," which, in its purest form, is word of mouth marketing. "Hey didja read the new book that says you only have to work a few hours per week and you can get rich? Shoot even if I had to work twice that many hours that would still only be one day per week."

It is very easy to write an article that says you only have to work 10 hours per week to become a millionaire or financially free. It is quite another thing to make that happen in reality.

So, what would working a few hours a week really look like? Imagine that you did start a home business today. Let's put in five hours this week. It will take approximately five hours to do a name search for your new business, get your tax forms from the Internal Revenue Service, get your tax ID number assigned, file your incorporation forms with your state, send in your registration fee, and jump through a few other administrative hoops.

The next week, you open your business bank account. From the time you leave home until the time you return is about two hours. It should only take a few minutes but bankers love to make you wait, then sit and talk and talk. You sign more forms now than you used to before September 11th. You stop at the store on your way home and pick up files and a cabinet. You'll need to grab a nice printer for your home computer and probably a fax/phone answering machine. You get home, and begin your filing system for your new company and you have to call it a day. You also call the phone company to have them come by next week during your half day of work (good luck) for installation. Time's up.

Next week it is time to attach your printer to the computer and get your new phone line installed. You will be at home for a half-day window for most phone installers. The process is quick—normally less than an hour or so. But the waiting is a different story. Nevertheless you can fire up the computer and buy a program to build your web site (or open an eBay account or whatever start-up stuff is necessary for your new home business). If you are good at multitasking you can get your software installed. If you completely lack basic skills, you can farm out the creation of your web site and purchasing and installation of your software to someone else and let them have access to all of your money.

Time's up.

The following week, you learn the basics of your newly purchased software or start posting stuff on eBay or whatever it is you are going to do. It will take you four hours to learn the basics of most software programs if they come with video tutorials. And many do. Time's up.

The next week you create passwords for your new accounts. You buy a store for your web site or create a store for your eBay site. As a rule it takes about 10 hours to set up a store for your web site assuming everything goes smoothly, which it will about one-third of the time. Again, you can outsource all of this to someone else, but then they will have access to your money. This is a risk many intelligent business people aren't willing to take. But if you did choose to outsource this, it would take you four hours of research to find someone competent, do a credit check, a background check, and hire him. Time's up.

Now you have a rudimentary web site or your eBay store set up.

Okay . . . is the point clear yet? It takes about 50 hours to begin the simplest of businesses.

Online businesses are a huge gift to those of us who may never have had a chance in the brick and mortar world. It's pretty easy to make a living on the Web. Much easier, anyway, than launching a brick and mortar business with all its attendant overhead costs, that is for sure. But the fact is, using the five-hour-per-week plan, it will take you three months just to launch your first product and make your first sale.

Our preference when starting a project or a business (and we've launched many) is to get it done in a few days. Just launch it as quickly as possible instead of spreading the work out over a few months.

Once you start your new business, whether online or off-line, you will need to put money into your marketing effort. You can have a beautiful web site, a gorgeous McDonald's or Curves franchise, but if you do not market, well, you will be flat out of luck.

Yes, you could farm out the marketing as you launch a new store or new Internet business. But that process is not going to happen in 20 hours. And do you really want to outsource the marketing of your new business? If you put $100,000 into a brick and mortar business, who, specifically, are you going to hire to promote that business, given that you need to turn a profit instantly to start paying the bank back? And if you are online, who are you going to hire to market your business? How do you know that individual is talented, creative, and able to do it successfully for you? How will you pay for those services?

Success Actions That Work: If you use a five-hour workweek to start your own business on the Internet, it could take you up to a year before you begin to make a profit. It will take you the rest of your life in a brick and mortar business.

Now, is the idea of outsourcing work a good one? You bet.

Carefully identify people you trust to help you with parts of your business that you lack expertise in and try to figure out a way to pay them from profits if you lack up-front money. Most won't do that unless you have a proven track record in business. In that case, you will need to build your business over time, stash some cash, and then begin outsourcing in a year or two.

There are a lot of things in business you can barter, too. For example, if you help me with my web site I might help you create a joint venture with a bunch of people to help market your new business. No money required, but you do need time.

Finally, if you already have plenty of money, many of the problems are solved. You still have to get the paperwork to the bank. No one can open your bank account for you anymore. But if you are already wealthy then you ought to be outsourcing more and more work as time goes on. That could mean hiring or using temporary help.

The concept of a short workweek is good. The dream is incredible. The reality is that the dream will come true but it will take time—your time—to make it happen.

Question: **From hearing you speak, I know that you are a self-made success story. You started without money and are now a millionaire. What was the biggest mental attitude you had to change or adapt to allow yourself to feel worthy of having money?**

First, no one is completely self-made. We've all had mentors, partners, and other support along the way. So if you are trying to go it alone on your path to wealth, you will want to revisit that strategy.

The biggest deterrent to financial success that we see is fear. Many people who have money problems fear losing money so much that they actually aggravate their problems by concentrating too much on them. They can't think of any solution to their dilemmas because their thoughts are preoccupied with the terror of paying what they see as an insurmountable pile of bills.

For the poor and middle class, the fear of losing money makes them cringe when considering taking risks, even the calculated risks that the rich typically take. Sometimes, they never realize that they have already lost the moment they back out from an opportunity. And if this continues, they will never be secure.

Fear has its good side. A little fear can prevent us from getting hurt, physically and emotionally. It prevents us from being too aggressive. It makes us think before we act. Action after thinking is definitely better than action without thinking. But uncontrolled fear leads to poverty. It prevents financial creativity and puts our minds in disarray. Unconsciously, we become greedier.

So how do you control fear from overwhelming you? How do you keep fear to a manageable and usable level so you have control over it instead of the other way around?

To effectively suppress the fear of losing money, the excitement of winning must prevail. And winning is addictive.

You must have the burning desire and the passion to make it happen. To help fuel that burning desire, think of the great benefits that money will bring. "What will I do or what can I do when I become wealthy?"

Practice feeling wealthy. Experience it in your mind as if you're already enjoying the lifestyle you desire.

Now, play along here . . .

Really imagine what life would be like if you were wealthy. Don't just see it. Feel it. You are enjoying all of the luxuries of the rich and famous. Make it a complete picture.

See yourself in the surroundings you want to be in with the kind of people you want to be with. Visualize the things you would like to do with money. Concentrate first on the good things it will bring to you and your loved ones, perhaps helping a younger sibling finish college or going on a big family vacation cruise if you love to travel, or taking care of a loved one's medical expenses. Acts of care and concern, not only for oneself and family, but for others as well, ignite passion and desire. Compassion puts your creative mind to work.

Go ahead and visualize a house that might be cool to have as your own. How many rooms does it have? What do the master bedroom and bathroom look like? Take a relaxing soak in the hot tub. What features are included in the kitchen? See yourself in the kitchen gathered with family or friends. What types of recreation are important to you? See yourself working out in your private gym, shooting baskets on your court, or lounging by your swimming pool.

The important thing here is to see yourself living the life without spending the money.

Got a clear picture? Feel good? Are you reenergized and ready to get to work?

By doing this exercise, you are coding into your unconscious mind a bit of a direction. You are encouraging it to move you in the direction of your dreams. Begin doing this daily to help keep you on the right path. A few years down the road, you may be astounded at how closely your life mirrors the image that you begin building in your mind today. Not because you attracted your results, but because you established a direction and opened yourself up to see new opportunities.

Success Actions That Work: You cannot create your future simply by visualizing it. But you can use visualization exercises to code a direction into your unconscious mind directing it to move you toward what you're dreaming of. Wealth building also requires putting your thoughts into action by making big but realistic and detailed step-by-step plans.

Step into your wealth. Find ways to try on the wealthier you. Indulge in experiences that make you feel as if you're already living your desired life. For example, instead of going out to dinner several times next month, go to dinner once at a very nice restaurant and take a limo. Think, "I could get used to this." Reward yourself for working hard and embrace your right to enjoy the fruits of your labor. Try on wealth in small ways and gradually move on to bigger activities. Have fun with this and use it to energize your progress!

On your path to wealth, remember to be grateful and to be generous with your riches.

Be Grateful

Be grateful you were born in a free country.

Be grateful that you can dream a dream that can become reality when so many cannot even do that.

Be grateful for all of your talents, abilities, and potential.

Everyone has strengths. Identify yours, use them, and be grateful for them.

Be grateful for your opportunities.

Be grateful that you did the right things to get you where you are.

By being thankful for your opportunities and for the decisions you have made, you are confirming that you are graciously accepting your life experience. You are acknowledging that you have earned what you have. No matter where you are right now, you can find some things to be grateful for.

As your wealth grows, so should your sense of gratitude. Yes, you deserve what you have earned. Being grateful means accepting that you are no better than anyone else. It's essential that you never lose sight of how you got what you have. None of us becomes successful without the help of others. Be grateful for each good decision, action taken, bit of help received, and result produced along the way.

As you build your wealth, continue to enjoy the fruits of your hard work, be grateful for them, and share them with others.

Be Generous

Rich people are selfish, that's why they have lots of money at hand. Right? Nope.

This may be true in some cases, but there are a lot more individuals who are wealthy because they know how to give. And we are not just talking about charitable acts.

The wealthy contribute mightily to the tax base. They pay disproportionately for the services that keep our country running and in fact, those of many other countries. The top one percent of wealthy people in the United States pay nearly 40 percent of the income taxes collected each year and the top two percent pay well more than half of all the expenses it costs to run the country. And then they go further. It would take tens of thousands of ordinary people to match what Bill Gates and Oprah Winfrey have given to millions of disadvantaged people over the years. Wealthy people grow their wealth through a spirit of generosity.

Whenever possible, be generous with others. Research shows that what you receive back (emotionally, spiritually, and even in physical health benefits) will be worth more than what you give.

It is a paradox of giving. The payoff of giving can feel selfish. It feels good to hear recipients express heartfelt gratitude and to see their smiles extend from ear to ear. Think of it as one of life's inherent win-win situations.

Give something from your heart without expecting anything in return. This opens the door to a powerful mind-set that will trigger your mind to act as if you are capable of performing that behavior again and again. Give wisely (learn from any bad decisions along the way.) And give freely. Do not get into a habit of thinking of reciprocation when you give or you are destined to feel resentment and anger.

Try giving anonymously. Give without saying anything. For instance, adopt a family at Christmastime. Give them food, clothes, gifts, toys—whatever you are capable of giving. Play Santa Claus in secret. Experience the joy of giving. Experience the value of making a difference. Do this just once and you will be forever addicted to the feeling. It's one of the best feelings you will ever experience.

There is little research on anonymous giving. This is personal experience: When you give secretly, you feel a true and good power inside. You have a strength to help and care for others. You believe in yourself more. You have more self-confidence. You know that your behaviors match your words and beliefs.

If you work for the sole purpose of making money, you will have a harder time creating wealth. And you definitely will enjoy it less.

Starting now, begin a habit of generosity. Give what you can. What you give does not necessarily have to be something material. It can also be time, effort, talent, service, or even an affectionate feeling.

Use your wealth to make a difference. Enjoy this process. It will motivate you to create more and more wealth . . . so you can keep giving more to others.

11

Support
Structures

A high level of achievement requires that you put significant support structures in place. Successful people understand the need to go beyond themselves and rely, in part, on others for their success. Every person has different skills, talents, and abilities that when combined with those of others, lead to an individual's success. It will always take more time, effort, knowledge, and resources for you to achieve success by yourself.

We need to heed the judgments of others. The fact is other people can see a lot about you that you can't see yourself. We need people to see if we are succeeding or failing. We need to be *accountable*. We often need to pick the brains of other people. Success is much easier to achieve if you have people on your side.

The need for support structures grows as you become even more successful. The reason is very simple. Once you've reached one level of success it is very likely that you'll immediately strive for another. Or, as you reach milestones in your quest for success in an area, you'll expand your definition of what success you want. The result is that your need for support structures grows.

Humans crave connection with others. This doesn't change in the pursuit of success. Personal relationships fulfill our psychological and biological needs to connect to others and are important to a fulfilling life. Successful people understand this and make the effort to actively cultivate additional relationships to support their success. These kinds of relationships are primarily cultivated for the purpose of providing additional assistance in reaching one's goals.

Although success often feels like a singular effort, it rarely is. In fact, most success is a series of large and small moves fueled by the contributions of many. While there are countless stories about the athlete who always went to practice before anyone else got there, that individual likely had support of some sort from coaches, teammates, family, and others. When the going gets tough and you are losing focus, it is a great boost to have someone you can turn to and get a little push.

Relationships, both formal and informal, can significantly enhance your chances of success while reducing the time needed to achieve success. One of the fastest routes to success is to build on the experiences and successes of others who willingly support you. The better you become at cultivating and leveraging relationships the better your odds are of achieving success.

All connections you make with people may offer some support of your success, but all relationships are not equal. Three of the most useful support structures to develop are mastermind groups, your personal network, and accountability partners.

Mastermind Groups

The term "mastermind" was first introduced by the late Napoleon Hill in his book *Think and Grow Rich*. Hill defined the mastermind principal as: "The coordination of knowledge and effort of two or more people, who work toward a definite purpose, in the spirit of harmony." Mastermind groups are most often found in the world of business but exist in coordinated endeavors to create change everywhere.

A lot of confusion exists about what a mastermind group is. Let's start by clarifying some common misunderstandings.

1. A mastermind group is not a psychological support group. The idea of connecting, sharing ideas, and providing reinforcement to one another is similar. Support groups have been shown to help members who are active in their commitment to the effort and to the group. A significant difference between the two types of groups is that mastermind groups typically support moving *toward* ideas while support groups often support moving away from ideas. For example, the international Entrepreneurs' Organization is moving toward the idea of providing a place where entrepreneurs can share the best experiences and ideas for growing businesses. Alcoholics Anonymous supports keeping people from drinking.

2. A mastermind group is not a personal support group. A working personal support group is essential to success. It will help you with the implementation of your strategy and help you keep going through the setbacks you'll experience along the way. This group includes friends, family, staff, and volunteers who will do whatever is necessary for you to achieve your success. When putting together this group, think of what Thomas Edison said. "I have friends in overalls whose friendship I would not swap for the favor of the kings of the world." Look for this in your personal support group. Look for the ones who are willing to show up in overalls and lend a hand. These are the friends who matter. They will help you achieve anything.

3. A mastermind group is not the same as a fraternity or a social organization like Jaycees or Kiwanas, or a church group. While

you may find very effective mastermind partners in these types of groups, they are not typically organized to help you actively move forward in your goals. These groups are organized for a different purpose, often around philanthropy or social interaction. This being said, social groups and business groups can be an important success structure. They provide an opportunity to expand your network. Everyone seeking business, financial, or career success should constantly be expanding his network.

4. A mastermind group is not simply a brainstorming group, although brainstorming can be a process that your mastermind group uses. Brainstorming is a creativity technique and term originated by Alex Osborn in the 1930s as a group problem solving process. (Osborn is the O in the advertising agency BBDO.) What passes for brainstorming in most groups is simply just an idea dump. Osborne's process is specific. If you are interested in better understanding the brainstorming process, pick up a copy of his book *Applied Imagination: Principles and Procedures of Creative Problem Solving* (Osborn 1963) to learn the process from the originator. It is very powerful.

So, what is a mastermind group? It is a structured group that is organized around a common theme and purpose and focused around the specific needs and information exchange that happens between like-minded people who have similar business goals. The purpose of having like-minded people in the group is to support continued thinking about a subject without losing interest. It is also to provide ongoing support and accountability for the members. A key to masterminding success is to have clearly defined questions. Clearly defined questions are fast attractors of powerful solutions.

Masterminds provide several key supports that allow you to achieve success and to achieve it faster. First, being able to discuss your goals or challenges with like-minded, experienced people gives you an opportunity to get feedback critical to your success.

Second, ideas and solutions tend to grow exponentially when exposed to group thinking and interaction. Finally, there is an accountability loop, which helps increase the likelihood of success.

An effective mastermind will help you grow your strengths. You will learn from the combined experience and wisdom of the group. Your perspective will expand as you begin to see yourself, your challenges, and your opportunities from another's point of view. You will receive vital support as you move toward achieving your goals and dreams. You will create a synergy that catapults each member to greater levels of success much more quickly than anyone could have attained it on his own.

Social Networks

Social networking has recently taken on a whole new meaning. Until about 2006, social networks were the sum total of people in your Rolodex or address book—personal and professional relationships you'd developed over time. Around 2006, all that started to change with the advent of Myspace.com, Facebook.com, LinkedIn.com, and other online social networking tools. The initial idea for these groups was to connect people's offline social networks online. What has resulted instead is a massive interconnected web that has turned into a very viable marketing tool and yes, a means of connecting with those people in our actual offline networks.

Success is often dependent not on who you know but who the person you know can introduce you to. Developing a network of friends, acquaintances, and business connections is one of the fastest ways to achieve the success you are looking for. The more minds you can connect with, the more likely you'll be able to quickly identify and get an introduction to the person who can best help you.

Clarity is the basis of a good connection so start by getting clear about why you want to connect with someone. It is time well spent to make a complete list of all the people you'd like to be able to connect with, either in person or online. Are you sure you have identified the right person to help you? How do you know? Is there anyone else who would be better or perhaps as good but easier to reach?

Once you have decided you want to connect with someone it's time to get to know a bit more about them. Even if you have a connection who will introduce you, it is mandatory that you do your research in advance. With the avalanche of information available online, the proliferation of blogs, and easy access to media sites you should be able to find out something meaningful about the individual that you can use as an ice breaker or to develop rapport easily.

If you do not have a connection through another person, then start looking for personal e-mail information so that you can connect online. Leverage the information that you have discovered to ask a question about a passion, hobby, or other interest. Your goal should be to initiate a conversation that doesn't involve asking for help. The key to success is to develop a relationship over a series of conversations before asking for help. If you ask for help the very first time you meet, especially if it is through e-mail, it is too easy for your new acquaintance to say no. If, however, you develop a relationship first you greatly increase your chance of success.

Accountability Partners

People who are legitimately accountable to another person who proactively supports them are more likely to succeed than those who are not held accountable. Athletes have coaches and many executives have managers or mentors. Do you have someone to hold you accountable as you are trying to achieve your goals? If not, make arrangements with another person to hold each other accountable or hire a professional coach to serve this pivotal support role.

Take actions to tell your mind that you are taking account-ability seriously. Actually sign a contract giving the other person permission and authority to hold you accountable to your desired results. Being accountable to another is a powerful tool. It gives you a reason to move forward and it gives you a built-in emotional support person. This person will be your cheerleader, a coach who provides honest feedback and suggestions for staying on course, and an accountability partner who holds you to your word and enforces consequences when you don't do what you say you will. Before you know it, you'll need that person less than when you started out. But it's a good idea to always have this kind of person on your team to help keep you moving forward.

In order to make accountability effective, you need to tell your partner what specifically you want to be held accountable for. Decide what being accountable means. If your goal is to lose weight, then ask that your partner hold you accountable for exercising 30 minutes a day three times a week and following your chosen eating program or for losing a realistic amount of weight each week. Will your partner call you once a week? Or will you call or e-mail your partner? Be specific and make your progress measurable.

Probably the most overlooked aspect of accountability is the *consequence*. To increase the chances for success, you have to have a vested interest in creating the success. Set up something that hurts a little if you don't meet your end of the bargain. And follow through. The minute you don't pay your penalty for nonperformance, all accountability goes away and there is no reason to continue the process. Being accountable to yourself by setting up a penalty that you pay is not nearly as effective (because it is too easy to cheat) as having someone else to be accountable to.

When you decide the penalty for not taking the actions that you want to be held accountable for, give thought to using a consequence that will also motivate your accountability partner to hold you to the fire. For example, one of the authors once agreed to donate $100 to the charity of his accountability partner's choice each time he failed to meet the prescribed actions. It was a very motivating experience and it kept the other party involved too because the partner wanted money for his charity (and he got about $500 before the excuses stopped and real action started!)

When you don't meet your commitment to another person it will typically initiate a conversation that can be supportive. Having to admit failure can be a big driving factor in not failing again. These conversations, especially when conducted with someone who knows you well or a coach who has professional expertise, also can provide insights that you can use to build future success.

At their core, support structures like mastermind groups, personal net-works, and accountability partners are about fueling momentum with sup-port and accountability.

When you regularly implement the success factors set forth in this book, you will create momentum. You start regularly completing and accomplishing small things and these lead to bigger and bigger successes. This type of momentum is a state of mind. It's a way of life. You must live there to be really successful in all areas of your life.

Support structures can help you set a higher and higher level of course of action that will force you to build momentum at quicker speeds. High achievers understand that momentum can stop and sometimes even reverse itself. This is why they choose to surround themselves with others who will help keep them on track and moving forward.

Question: I am part of a small group of people who wants to start a local mastermind group that will meet monthly. What are the key things we need to put in place to ensure the success of our group and its members?

Good for you to give thought upfront to what your group will look like. The effort that you spend defining and developing your mastermind will largely determine the effectiveness of the group and its value to you. Here are some important factors for you to consider when putting together your group.

Purpose: Your mastermind group should have a definite purpose. Meeting without a clear purpose in mind only leads to meetings that go nowhere. Because your group will be made up of key and influential players, you must respect their time and commitment by letting them know exactly what you need from them and what they can expect to get in return.

Membership: Determine who should be a part of the group. You may discover a potential mastermind member anywhere, which is one reason to maintain a broad network. It is important to have like-minded people, that is, people who have similar yet diverse styles of thinking and experiences. It is also important that the members of the group be interested in being active participants. If someone is unwilling to participate by attending meetings and by sharing experiences and ideas in the group, then choose someone more committed for your group. It is important that there are no conflicts of interest, competitors (if a business group), or issues where anyone is concerned about confidentiality. Mastermind groups work best when people feel completely comfortable sharing information.

It is also important to understand that your mastermind group is not a place to have people who don't have something to offer everyone else in the group. This is not a place to bring in people and bring them along. The mastermind is a place for people of equal experience, stature, and needs to support each other. The problem of bringing in someone of unequal stature or experience is that the individual can't contribute or doesn't receive what he needs from the group. It is important that there is a regular, reciprocal exchange of information.

Structure: Define the structure of the group, when it will meet, for how long, what the process is for meeting, and who will play what roles at each meeting. An ideal size for an effective mastermind group is six to eight people. This ensures enough diversity in the group to provide a variety of experiences and enough needs that the group does not get stale. Your plan to meet once a month is good (and can be increased to twice a month if there are more pressing needs.) More frequent meetings are ineffective and can cause rapid fallout in the group because of issues related to time. Also, it is best not to hold your mastermind groups in public places due to the potentially confidential nature of information that may be discussed during your meetings.

One of the big mistakes people make when putting together a mastermind group is that they do not structure the process. When there is no structure and no one has specific responsibilities, it becomes a chat session that often doesn't have any valuable outcome. Here is a suggested structure for your group:

- For each meeting, identify one person who will discuss his project or needs. That person will be responsible for clearly identifying his goal, his project, the challenge and his particular needs.
- Allot approximately 30 minutes for that person to describe his situation. Once the description is done, give everyone else in the group five minutes each to ask clarifying questions.
- Move around the room and ask everyone to share their experiences, resources, and actual solutions that they've applied in the past to the problem at hand. If problem solving is required, then move through possible solutions. Allow the person who is presenting his project, goal, or needs to ask any additional questions of each person after that person provides his experiences or solutions.
- After you've gone around the room, particularly if the issue was one of problem solving, go back through and give everyone a chance to add anything that may have occurred to them after hearing the feedback from everyone else.

- Take a 10- to 15-minute break so that everyone can clear their head. This step is crucial and can be scheduled into each meeting.
- Reengage and cover any other topics that need to be covered by the group.

Cost: For a formalized personal mastermind group charging typically isn't required. But it also isn't uncommon to have some costs associated with the group. Those costs often revolve around a meeting space if you can't use one of the member's spaces, coffee or snacks, and fees for specialized speakers or information.

Consider charging a membership fee and decide how you would invest it. A very successful group one of the authors belonged to had a monthly fee of $100 per member and an eight-member cap on group size. That netted $9,600 per year, which provided plenty of money to hire a speaker twice a year to address the group and to pay for all of the incidentals including a Christmas party. There is certainly no reason to charge any fees if you don't want to but it does offer some additional flexibility in terms of what additional impact and information you can bring to the group.

Success Actions That Work: Use the above tips to clarify your mastermind group's purpose, membership requirements, structure, and fees. To support a thriving mastermind group over time, you have to know when to hold'em and know when to fold 'em. As you and your group mature and your needs or goals change, people will move on and you will find it necessary to add new people to your group.

It is important that you surround yourself with the people who can best assist you in reaching your goals. Everyone grows at a different pace. You may not always be a good fit for the group if its members evolve past you or vice versa. To best serve the group, everyone needs to know when to leave or when to mix up the group. The best sports teams in the world know when it is time to trade or retire players in order to move forward. Take a cue from their success to increase yours.

When done right, masterminding is a powerful success tool to help people who are already achieving at a high level take their performance even higher. Go to Bestsuccessfactors.com for more information about masterminding and other support structures.

Question: **What are the biggest mistakes you see people make when networking?**

The biggest mistake people make is not engaging and missing opportunities to network. You are surrounded by opportunities and sometimes these are one-shot deals. If you've only got one chance at getting someone to help you, *ask them.* What is the worst that can happen? You already know the answer. They could say no. In our experience, if you sincerely acknowledge another person and try to build a connection with them, they rarely will choose not to talk to you.

For instance, you happen to meet someone on an airplane, in a hotel, or at an event and you think he might be helpful in your future. After introducing yourself and building whatever rapport you can quickly, ask a connecting question. Say something like, "I've been wondering, who was the hardest person for you to get a connection to that you knew would have the biggest impact on your life or career and how did you make it happen?" When he tells you, compliment him on his creativity or determination. Then say, "I have a similar challenge—may I ask your advice?" Then ask your question. You've got one shot to get it right so be prepared when your opportunity comes along.

If possible, develop a reason to know the other person. Fire up your Blackberry or call your office for some quick research. Introduce yourself, use your connecting information, and go from there. Be brief, to the point, exchange information, and then follow up after the meeting with a handwritten note or a brief message. As authors, we often offer to send contacts a book as a means of getting their information. Think about what you have of value that you can offer to send. Then follow through.

Success Actions That Work: We see a lot of mistakes made as people try to network. Here is some advice to help you avoid these mistakes.

Do not ask for too much or too soon. You are much more likely to receive assistance or agreement to help if what you ask for can be provided quickly and easily. If you want someone to mentor you, ask them to mentor you on a very specific topic not be a mentor in general. Try and narrow it down to something the individual can do in an e-mail or with one short phone call. Once someone has agreed to do one thing, they are much more likely to agree to do another or to recommend that you talk again. Offer to follow up with them and let them know how their advice or their connection helped you. People often enjoy having closure around things they help initiate or create.

Do not fawn over the other person. We see people practicing too much hero worship when they make a high-level contact in an attempt to build a connection. Don't think that flattering the person you hope will help you is a sure way in. Your motive is often transparent and can work against you. Build rapport by asking relevant and considered questions.

Do not air your grievances. No one wants to help you when they see that you went out of your way to find them and complain. There will be a time and place to bring up your complaints. Leverage the relationship for something better. The only exception is if you are leveraging a relationship in order to connect with someone so you can try and solve a problem. Feel free to do this, but be sure that the person introducing you knows what you intend to do.

Do not ask too often. The thing that makes a network work is reciprocity. Take a little, give a little more than you get, and then ask again when you really need it. Someone who is always taking more than he gives or constantly asking for more will soon be shut out of any network.

Leave your gossip at home. Gossiping is not building rapport. It is letting the other person know that you can't be trusted. No one wants to run the risk that you soon will be talking about them to others. Build rapport on real information not idle gossip.

Last, but not least, stay in touch. You cannot expect much if you choose to not stay in touch and then ask for help out of the blue. Relationships are two-way streets. Be sure that you stay in touch with those with whom you want a business relationship to blossom.

Question: How do I best use online social networks to grow my business? Or do you think these are a waste of time?

Social networking online is harder than you might imagine. You probably have many people in your network who do not know a thing about you. Your friends on Facebook.com aren't really friends in the true sense. The majority of them probably couldn't tell you one meaningful thing about you. You simply met on Facebook and that doesn't really mean anything.

So the question is why become online friends with others? There are a couple of good reasons. One, if someone interesting invites you to be a friend, you then have permission to develop a relationship based on that connection. Second, the more people who get to know you, the larger your prospective market is. In our case, the more likely they are to buy our books or come to our events. So, go ahead and share information with them. You may want to go a step further and make them feel special by giving them access to information before you give it to anyone else. You can use online networking to create a sort of relationship that works for both parties while everyone is aware that they don't have to do much to keep the relationship alive.

Now, if you want to really leverage your online social network, you have to give more than you receive. You have to actively engage people in conversation. You have to ask about them, get to know them, and give them things that you don't give to others. Does this sound familiar? It sounds a lot like off-line networking, doesn't it? You're right. The rules don't change because the medium does. When you develop your network online, the best relationships will naturally evolve off-line.

As true with all networking, clarity is the basis of a good connection. Start by being clear about why you are connecting with someone. How are they going to help you become more successful? What exactly do you want them to do for you? Is there anyone else that might better help you achieve your goal?

Do your homework. Your objective is to find information that will give you insight into the things that they are interested in that can serve as a foundation for your connection. Begin searching the obvious—company web site, Google, and their local newspaper. Then search blogs (you can start your search at technorati. com or blogsearch.google.com). Look for passions, commitments to charities, school affiliations, civic affiliations, political affiliations, hobbies, or anything that you can use to connect and build rapport.

The real value of online networking is the ease with which you can connect with people. Most people don't understand this. They simply sense that they should be doing it so they fill out the forms and put themselves online. We predict that if people don't begin to leverage the power of online networking, it will lose its popularity. People will simply decide to take down their Facebook or other online pages because they don't use them to build relationships. Reading an online profile does not constitute a relationship.

Success Actions That Work: If you want to achieve success faster and build your network faster, study what is happening online (by the time you read this book it will have evolved). Get involved, connect with those people online who meet your needs, and actually work on developing a relationship. If they are not interested or if they are not a good match, get them out of your network and get out of theirs. You'll both be doing each other a tremendous favor.

One of the biggest values of online social networking is that you can connect with a lot of people who you'd normally never have access to and you already have the social networking platform in common. Beginning your relationship is easier because you can start by talking about the platform and your experiences of being involved. We have successfully used online connections (usually followed up by phone calls) to develop business relationships and even friendships. You can, too.

Question: I've heard that it is necessary to have people of all different economic, educational, and experiential levels in a mastermind group to make it most effective, is that true?

No, this is not true. While on the surface having people who have very broad economic, educational, and experiential levels in a group seems to make sense, it is actually detrimental. The problem is that the people who are most likely to support you are people most like you. When there is a marked difference in income levels, education levels, or experience levels an even exchange becomes impossible. Those people with the most experience end up being mentors to the group giving more than they receive and often quickly lose interest.

Another challenge when there are large differences in education or experience is that there tends to be a large passage of time since the other person faced the situation you are currently trying to solve. Often information that worked a few years ago is outdated (especially with the speed of progress we experience today.) But, when people who experience the same kinds of problems have solved them, they typically have real-world, recent, relevant solutions or ideas to share.

Large economic differences quickly can undermine the effectiveness of a mastermind group. When there are large economic differences between people, solutions that are available at one level may not be available at another. For example, solving a problem may be a simple financial decision for someone with a high six-figure income but impossible for someone who is making mid five figures.

If having someone who has significantly more experience, a larger income, or significant or specialized education would be helpful, invite them to come to a special meeting of your group. Build the meeting around the need and get the information from the person. Pay them if you must, but often they'll be happy to help without charge when there is no long-term commitment of their time. There are many good reasons to have highly skilled people available to your group but having them in the group will encourage frequent turnover and nearly always either kill the group because of a lack of equal or consistent participation.

Success Actions That Work: We are not saying that you want to compile a group of people who think exactly alike or so much alike that they don't challenge each other. You want your mastermind group to be filled with independent thinkers who are willing to speak their minds and challenge each other as needed. But to increase your chances of a successful mastermind group, make sure that these independent thinkers share common economic, educational, and experiential levels.

The one exception to this rule that often works out well is when you have a person in your group who is retired. Those people typically don't have an equal business need for reciprocal information. They can give more while still getting their needs met. Oftentimes, they want to participate for the camaraderie, to stay current in certain areas, or simply to make a contribution that makes them feel valued. There are many retired people who would be a tremendous asset to your group and shorten the amount of time and effort needed to achieve the success you are looking for, so do not overlook this valuable resource!

Question: How do I know when I'm ready to join a mastermind group? I am serious about my personal development and am ready to make some changes in my life, but I don't have a solid track record of success yet. I think I'd really feed off the energy of other go-getters but don't want to hold anyone back. Do I sound like a good mastermind candidate?

You do not necessarily need a solid track record of success, but you do need to have forward momentum to both take from and *give to* a mastermind group. Are you now doing things and completing projects every day that are moving you forward in the direction you have set for yourself? If you truly have set a course of action and are getting things done, then it is possible that an entry-level mastermind group would be a good support structure to help you continue building momentum.

From the wording of your question, it is our sense that you may need more self work before you are ready to successfully participate in a mastermind group. Do you believe that a high level of success and momentum is for other people but not you? That is a real question. Think about it before giving a knee-jerk answer. If your answer is yes, then no mastermind group is going to be your key to success. The answers to your success don't lie "out there," they lie within you.

Make it your job to figure out why you don't have a solid track record of success and fix those things that have been holding you back. If you've got a pessimistic attitude about what you can accomplish, begin trying to see how you are going to face each situation or opportunity. If you lack confidence, begin building a stronger belief in yourself and your potential. Take your personal development seriously. It's helpful to be objective while defining your goals and preparing your strategy, but the importance of your aspirations and goals in the big picture of your life should be a very personal matter indeed. Take it seriously and take it personally.

If you experience a setback, question why it happened. Did you try to take a shortcut instead of giving your full effort to a task? Did you make mistakes that caused a setback to occur? If so, internalize those insights and use them to avoid similar mistakes in the future. Hold yourself accountable for your actions going forward. Get back on track by doing more of what you need to do and less of what you've done in the past. It you continue to struggle, it may be helpful to hire a coach to help you set a personal action plan and hold you accountable to your plan.

To create forward momentum, you need to truly understand that failure flat out doesn't matter. It really doesn't. If we write a book and it doesn't become a big seller, are we disappointed? You bet. We have egos just like you. But what does this mean in the scope of history of the human race? *Nada*. The fact is that a lot of things you do are going to fail. And it does not matter.

Success Actions That Work: Creating success through personal development and goal achievement is very much a process of evolution. You first must open your mind to the possibilities, learn through self-discovery, take action and continually test your limits. If you take both of these processes personally, you will hold them close to your heart and place immense importance on them, which means you'll keep working toward them as long as it takes to make them a reality.

The more you work on yourself, the more motivated you will become to keep doing so. And as you improve as a person, so will your dreams and goals begin to grow larger and fuel your motivation to continue.

If you find yourself struggling along the way, it can help to remind yourself that *your greatness is already within you*. There is nothing to wait for! Once you've decided on an objective, made your plans, and done all the preparation you can, there is nothing left to do but go for it.

As you take steps toward your goals, you may be surprised to learn that your inner greatness will begin to grow as a *result* of your moving forward not the other way around. The longer you hang back and allow yourself to be held captive by uncertainty, the more difficult it will be to take a step forward. Push yourself to move forward even though you don't really feel ready yet and you will grow in confidence with every step you take.

Obviously having someone hold you accountable would be helpful to you. Accountability is something everyone needs to have and take advantage of. If you come to the conclusion that you're not yet ready for a mastermind group, then seek out a mentor, coach, or accountability partner to provide support. Look for someone who emphasizes accountability and knows how to leverage it to create action and results.

The bottom line is that you will never realize your true greatness until you develop the courage to express it. As you do, it begins to expand and become the bigger part of who you are. The more you are willing to express and expand your greatness, the less you will feel frightened by things that are out of your control, and the more you will naturally focus on the things that are within your control. Use every little victory along the path to your goals to inspire you to keep going, keep daring, and keep achieving.

12 Success Mind

Success is not doing things that are risky for the rush or the glory; it is about fully experiencing the life you have, in your own skin, for your own reasons. It is about accomplishing your dreams and leaving nothing undone when you finish.

Much of success is an inner game. You have to develop a success mind. This is a way of thinking, a way of being, and a way of doing that drives you forward through the good times and the tough times. Success is about doing one more thing, exploring one more option or opportunity when everyone else has stopped. It is having the drive to keep track of what is working and what is not. It is a process of continually learning new information that you can apply to reach your goals. And, it is about constantly striving to newer and bigger challenges and rewarding yourself for reaching your goals.

Fear keeps many people from reaching their goals. Fear of failure, fear of hard work, fear of what other people will think, fear that they are not good enough, fear of success. The interesting thing is that these types of fears are learned. We practice them over and over again until they become our automatic response.

Research shows that we can overcome nearly all fears or at least significantly reduce our response to fears through education, conditioning, and exposure to the triggers of our fears. One of the most successful therapies for people who have phobias is to educate them, and, over time, expose them to the object of their fear in a safe, controlled environment and continue to lengthen the exposure over time.

The success mind understands that we fear things less the more we do them. Do not limit yourself by past negative experiences of trying new things or being rejected by others. These experiences are not a clear indication of future outcomes. You have to engage again and again in order to get what you want. Developing a process that allows you to face whatever fear you have that is holding you back is a clear path to becoming more confident and more successful.

The success mind is geared toward taking chances and gives itself permission to fail. Taking risks is one of the hardest things for people to do. It is easier to stay put than risk adversity or hardship. Yet, if you talk to any star athlete, entrepreneur, explorer, researcher, or inventor, they'll all tell you the same thing: They learned more from their failures than their successes.

In part, we are wired to avoid risk. Psychologists have found that people faced with a sure opportunity with a lower payoff are much more likely to take it than a riskier option that has significantly higher reward, even when the returns favor the higher risk option. Learning to take reasonable, calculated risks is a skill that you must develop in order to build an empowering success mind-set.

Somewhere over the past century, we as a society have moved from a pioneering, exploring breed to one of constantly reducing risk and taking the safe route. If our pioneering ancestors had not taken the risk of going West, we'd all still live in a small area of the East Coast and would never have discovered gold in California, oil in Wyoming, or the Grand Canyon. A lot of people who left for the West didn't make it. They perished in all manner of fighting, flood, fire, or sickness. But those who did achieved something amazing, something not a lot of other people would attempt.

Today, one of the biggest risks that stops people from taking action on their dreams and achieving their success has nothing to do with losing life, limb, or fortune. The risk that keeps many people from taking action on their dreams and doing what they must to get what they most want is worrying about what other people think. We repeatedly see how doing something (or not doing something) because of what a person thinks others might think keeps people broke, unhappy, and incomplete. People worry about what their friends will say, they worry that the neighbors will talk, they worry what complete strangers will think, and they worry that if they fail everyone will know.

The person who has developed a true success mind says, "So what?" At the end of the day, it doesn't matter what anyone thinks but you. Only you have to live with your success or your failure.

The most notable aspect of the success mind is that it understands that success favors action. Success without action is rare and it comes from luck. Lucky breaks do happen and they count for something, but they can't be counted on. The success mind focuses on leveraging experiences over time and continuously gaining more. As Buckminster Fuller said, "You can't learn less, you can only learn more." The success mind continues to do and learn and grow and expand.

Implementation is essential. The biggest successes in the world happen because someone *did something*. They kept learning from their mistakes or failures and kept moving forward. The belief that you have to start from a place of perfection is what keeps many people from achieving the success they dream of. The reality is that you don't have to get everything perfect, you just have to get started. You can't wait for ideal conditions because they rarely exist. You can't wait for perfect timing because it rarely comes. You simply have to make your decision, set your course, and take off. You can adjust along the way, you can gather new information, you can modify your goal as your knowledge changes, but you must take the first step.

The success mind allows itself to dream. It is constantly filled with many dreams. While success is in the action, possibility is in the dreaming. The success mind is powerful because of its ability to generate new ideas, new possibilities, and new dreams for you and for the world.

Take time to consider your dreams and dream big. Go beyond climbing a mountain or running a marathon. These types of goals are important for creating a full life and for having amazing experiences that will lead you to bigger thoughts. But we're talking about the dreams that will change your life and the lives of your family and friends—dreams that will change the world.

It is important that you regularly capture those dreams so that you can begin working on them. If nothing were impossible, what would you do? Very little is truly impossible. You just have not figured out how to do it yet. And, the thing you figure out may well be the thing that becomes your legacy. Think long-term, think big. Be a radical, a revolutionary, and a renegade when you think. Embrace what could be, what could define your life. Going after big dreams makes your current desires easier to reach.

Successful people and people who achieve great things believe in themselves. They believe that they are doing something meaningful and worthwhile. They hold onto their belief even after everyone else stops believing. That mental toughness, determination, and unwavering focus help them achieve what it is that they set out to do. Athletes often experience moments of sheer exhaustion and pain and still they push on. Many successful entrepreneurs push through a lack of funds, a lack of resources, a lack of support, and many other setbacks. They do it because they know in their hearts that they are doing the right thing and that they can win. And they do.

If your goal is important enough, if your dream is big enough, then have the courage to believe in yourself first. The success mind is about considering the facts and pushing forward with the best information available, creating new solutions as you go and staying your course no matter what. Believing in yourself is an individual effort first. Selling others on believing in you comes later and is much easier when you have developed a real and deep confidence in yourself.

Make a commitment here and now to develop your success mind today. It is never too late to develop your success mind and the time to stop developing it is never. Your thoughts, your feelings, your actions, your beliefs are the biggest predictors of your success. Develop a success mind by putting in place a solid structure that supports success and rewards your effort. Give yourself the room to experience and to fail. Develop a process for getting up one more time than you fail. Stop caring what other people think.

Most importantly, dream big and take consistent, directed, and smart action. Then use your success mind to evaluate the results, make corrections, redirect the effort, engage again, and refuse to quit. Do this and you will be on your way to greater success than you imagined possible.

Question: **What is more important for success: critical thinking or creative thinking?**

Both critical thinking and creative thinking are important parts of success thinking.

People often incorrectly believe that critical thinking and creative thinking are two opposing forces when in reality they are opposite sides of the same coin. Critical thinking leads to the skill that allows the artist to bring the creative masterpiece to life. As in most things, the goal is to find balance, the middle path where the two work in harmony and achievements happen quickly and easily.

When problem solving, use both critical thinking and creative thinking. It is important to creatively think the big thoughts first when you are solving a problem and then narrow them down critically. The point of critical thinking in creating your success is not to discount big ideas. It is to deduce from the information at hand what is possible now. Creative thinking will lead you to many solutions. It allows you to challenge the norm and develop paths to a higher norm. Critical thinking will lead you to the path that gets you there the quickest or to the path with the biggest payoffs.

On the creative thinking side, put a process in place to publish the contents of your mind. The success mind needs to be heard. It is important to capture your thoughts so that you can go back through them and connect the dots. Ideas that are not captured tend to fade with time. Journaling your thoughts and keeping a record of your thinking around your big ideas, your big goals, and your feelings of being successful will drive you further. A different kind of thinking emerges when you begin writing down the contents of your mind. If you don't like writing, draw them out, if you don't like drawing, speak them into a microphone. Whatever you do, record your thoughts. The thoughts of today are the fuel for tomorrow.

As an aside, remember to keep your journal where you will always find it. Choose a home for your journal and keep it there unless you are writing in it. Establishing a permanent place for your journal—under the bed, on the top shelf in the closet, in a dresser drawer, on your nightstand—is an important step in establishing a journaling routine. This not only will eliminate the possibility of losing your journal but will help reinforce permanence and form new habits.

On the critical thinking side, learn to question everything. Just because someone says something doesn't make it so. Just because it is written doesn't make it so.

For example, we hear a lot of talk about left-brain and right-brain people. And there is valid research to support this distinction. But there also are a lot of poorly equipped so-called experts who build a career on nonvalid assessments and an over exaggeration of this lateralization. We won't go into this in detail because we do not want to detract from the larger message here. And the message is this: Do not limit yourself by putting yourself in a box as a left-brain logical type or a right-brain creative type.

Your growth is not static and you will not achieve your highest level of success while being artificially constrained by some label. Brain research has moved beyond the years in which it was believed that your brain became hardwired at an early point in life. Recent research shows a very different picture. Brain plasticity lasts a lifetime. What this means to the success mind is that no matter when you start, as long as you stay focused and take action, learning and enhancing the skills that will help you reach and support your goals, you will build new supportive habits.

The research in this area is intriguing. For example, studies by Dr. Michael Merzenich, professor at the Keck Center for Integrative Neurosciences at the University of California, San Francisco, show the importance of ongoing learning and the effects of repeatedly practicing an activity (Deutschman 2007). In one study, rats were conditioned by getting a reward of food after solving a puzzle. After 100 trials, the rat solved the puzzle perfectly and after 200 trials, the rat could remember how to solve the puzzle for almost its entire lifetime. In another study, Dr. Merzenich used an MRI to examine brain patterns in highly trained individuals, including a professional flute player and a Buddhist monk who was exceptionally skilled at meditation. This study showed that these highly disciplined individuals actually distorted their brain over time. The professional flute player, for instance, had large representations in his brain in the areas that control the fingers, tongue, and lips.

This line of brain research confirms what we see all the time as we work with highly successful people. They simply think differently. And this success mind begins with choices and behaviors. So you do not need to choose between creative and critical thinking. Use both. And to reach your highest level of achievement, understand that disciplined practice is the key to building better habits. How exciting is that? You can *choose* to develop a success mind. And it is never too late to start!

Question: I have found a new level of success by saying no to things so that I can say yes to my true priorities. I have heard you talk about the "the power of yes." Is this what you are talking about?

Learning to say "no" to things that can sidetrack your success. is an important element of time management. You discipline yourself to say no to things so that you then can say yes to yourself and your true priorities. This is important.

When we talk about the power of yes, we actually are talking about a broader concept of consistently using the word "yes" to expand your opportunities, your world, and your success. The power of yes is a crucial part of the success mind. The power of yes means saying yes to opportunities when they arise. A big part of success is being present enough to recognize opportunity and to seize it by simply saying yes. The interesting thing about saying yes is that you can always say no later if it isn't what you needed or if it isn't getting you closer to your goal. But once you say no to an opportunity the opportunity is often gone and you may not get it back or if you do, it may not offer the same lesson or access.

The more you say yes to opportunities in your life the more opportunities you get. Not because you say yes, but because you condition your mind to see the opportunities all around you. Your mind will make the connections between your goals and your situations and present you with opportunities that can move you forward . . . if you'll just say yes.

The most successful people say yes to a wide variety of experiences and opportunities because the breadth of experience is what gives you a pool of knowledge from which to build powerful dreams and bulletproof action plans. When you've experienced much in life you can never flex back to a place of inaction. You always move forward. Once you've said yes and experienced what it will do for you, the idea of not having an experience becomes the most foreign thing you can imagine. This will propel you forward to new heights.

We each have stories of the opportunities brought to us by the power of yes. One of the most dramatic comes from Dave's background of being raised in a severe religious cult for ten years from the time he was six years old. Here is his story:

Within the cult, my family and I were systematically controlled. The group believed in an end time prophet named William Branham. They believed that he was the literal resurrection of the prophet Elijah from the Bible and the forebear of the apocalyptic interpretation of the Bible's Book of Revelation. Education past the sixth or seventh grade was not allowed. Women were not allowed to cut their hair, wear pants, wear makeup, or be disobedient to their husbands. There was no music that wasn't Christian music, no television, no movies. We were to minimize our contact with nonbelievers and to marry only other believers. My brother had ADHD and was believed to have the devil in him. He was regularly beaten to get the devil out of him. Church was Tuesday, Thursday, some Fridays, and twice on Sunday, and they were long fire-and-brimstone meetings.

Along the way, I realized that something was different about us. It struck me that maybe the rest of the world wasn't wrong, that maybe our view was somehow flawed. I rebelled by not leaving school after seventh grade and asking hard questions. And, along the way I paid a price for my disobedience. By the time I was 16 years old, I knew I had to leave home and my family to escape the church. I spoke to my mom and told her what I was going to do. When I went to the church one last time I was taken up front by the pulpit. The ministers and deacons laid their hands on me and prayed to God that he would turn my soul over to Satan for the destruction of my flesh, that I would be killed for my transgressions. And then I left.

This experience somehow developed within my mind the idea that I'd die by the time I was 25. I never put my finger on exactly where this idea came from, but I believed it completely. And in the moment I recognized this thought, I began fueling my success with the power of yes. I was going to use up every minute of my life and I wasn't going to leave anything undone. By saying yes, I was unknowingly developing a key component of the success mind.

And, when I say yes, I dive in. I question, challenge, think, experience, and form opinions. I don't just dip my toe in the water. I *dive* in. I don't read a book on the topic I read 30 or 40 books on the topic. I read research papers, I pick up the phone and call the thought leaders in the area and ask them questions. I want to know what they think about and how they came to their conclusions. And I keep getting deeper and deeper into the experience to understand how—if at all—it has application to me and my life.

My brother told me an interesting story. When he was in his twenties, he wanted to see what it was like to be homeless so he drove to San Francisco and stayed with the homeless people there for a few days. He lived with them during the day and slept with them at night. He had a very real experience. I asked him what he learned from the experience and for him it was that homelessness was never an option and that he needed to deepen his relationship with his family. You probably won't choose to go to this extreme. My brother is a real explorer (he climbs mountains for fun.) But once you put yourself in an experience, you can never see it the same way again. And that experience will oftentimes be the thing that sparks an idea that you can take action on that will make all the difference.

Success Actions That Work: Say yes to expanding your horizons. See how others live. Try on another perspective. Travel outside of your state and even your country. International travel will open your eyes to many new ideas and opportunities. It also will open your eyes to the challenges that people in other countries face that you many never have faced in your lifetime. Sure you can see it on television, but it isn't the same as seeing, feeling, touching, tasting, and smelling firsthand.

Many people will say, "I'd love to do that but I don't have the money." We are bordered by two very large countries that nearly anyone can get to. But even if you can't travel internationally, travel to a big city that has significant populations from other cultures; go to a Chinatown or Little India. If you can't do that, strike up a friendship with an immigrant and ask them to share their experiences of their homeland. You'll be amazed at what you learn and think about when you get a completely different perspective. Take a close look at the beliefs that have got them where they are or those that have kept their country from evolving.

Use this quote by Buckminster Fuller to remind you to say yes: "I'm not a genius. I'm just a tremendous bundle of experience." Saying yes increases the size of the bundle.

Question: I have had many goals in life and business and to date have met most of them. Yet, I have never felt like a success, because I quickly replace a met goal with a new one and this overwhelms any feeling of elation or success. My question is how do you know when you have truly succeeded?

First, know that you are in good company. We frequently get asked this type of question. There are many people out there trying to get ahead. They are working hard and are achieving at a higher and higher level. But they never really feel like they've made it. Over time, they begin to wonder if there really is such a thing as true success and, if so, what exactly does it look like.

In many ways, success is a journey, not a destination. Thus, there is not a single finish line. But there certainly are accomplishments along the way and an important part of success is acknowledging and celebrating these milestones. The success mind not only learns from its failures, but it also enjoys its successes.

One of the most important things that you can do when deciding on a goal or starting down a path is to clearly define success. Many people don't know what success looks like so they don't know when to quit. They keep going long after they've reached the goal because they didn't know what completion looked like. They just kept putting out the effort without looking at the result. You can't complete any task for which you don't have a definition of the finished product.

Measure your success. Do this by clearly defining what the end goal is, what success looks like and then by creating a path for getting there. Set up the timeline and the process and then measure your progress against that. Be honest with yourself when measuring actual effort you put into the process. In our experience, people commonly over estimate their time and effort. The reason is that they count all the time they are thinking and emoting and not acting by making some tangible effort. Thinking and taking action are not the same. Be honest about measuring your effort and you'll be much better able to measure your success.

In your case, it sounds like you have created a habit of glossing over achievement and celebration and simply jumping to the next goal. If so, you need to set up a time of feeling elation and a means of rewarding yourself. If you have clearly defined the goal, know that is has been reached, and success has been achieved, you need to celebrate it! No matter how big or how small the accomplishment, spend some time actually enjoying what it feels like to be successful.

Go ahead, gloat. Be happy for your victory. Reward yourself in a way that is meaningful and leaves a mark that you can remember. Accept awards, compliments, and accolades from those around you, your accountability partners, and your friends. It is good to take the praise you've earned and deserve.

You worked hard to achieve your goals. You were disciplined, made sacrifices, and got the job done. This effort shouldn't come without a reward. In order to continue a high level of motivation, you need to reward yourself appropriately for your accomplishment.

At a deeper level, when you achieve something important and then move right on to something else without acknowledging your victory, your life begins to lack meaning. You begin to lose sight of why you are doing what you do. In his book *Man's Search for Meaning,* Victor Frankl describes how Jews interned in concentration camps celebrated small victories and used these celebrations to keep going. They found meaning in everything they did and that meaning sustained them. You cannot gain sustenance from what you do not acknowledge and embrace. If you condition yourself to move on rather than reflect and enjoy, you lose the behavior of enjoying.

Success actions that work: Spend more time with your successes. You might find it helpful to record your successes in a journal. Talk about what it feels like to have achieved an important goal. Really experience it fully and write down everything about it. Write down what the voice in your head is saying. Write down what the feeling in your body is. Write down how you felt the moment you realized you'd succeed. Write down how you are going to reward yourself and how it felt to enjoy the well-earned reward.

Be sure to pick your rewards wisely. If you successfully diet and reach your goal weight, don't choose a reward of skipping a workout or eating the most fattening food that you enjoy. These would not be good rewards because they would reinforce the behavior that kept you from your goal, not the effort that helped you achieve it. A more productive reward might be putting on a swimsuit or bikini and spending some time by the beach or lake. Another option would be to buy a custom suit or the perfect little black dress. It is important that hard work comes with reward. We need to condition ourselves to experience a positive payoff for going through the effort.

So, if you feel like jumping up and down, do it! If you feel like downgrading your successes or hiding your pride of accomplishment, stop it! Success is to be savored. The more you let yourself experience how good it feels to succeed, the more you will be able to use the desire for that feeling to drive you forward.

Question: I've heard that people actually fear success more than they fear failure. Do you think this is true?

A fear of success just does not sound right, does it? Everyone can understand a fear of failure. After all, no one wants to be a loser. But fear of success? Yes, it is real. We see it all the time.

A fear of success can be confusing. You say you want to go to the top of that mountain, but as you get closer you really start to think about what it will be like.

Will you really be happy?

Will your life truly be complete?

Will you become lost and worried that there is nothing else to do and nowhere else to climb?

Will you be lonely?

Is it what you truly wanted?

Will you get to the top and feel like you made a mistake in your life?

A lot of times we are too stubborn to admit that we are afraid of success or of what it will bring us. So we lie to ourselves, thinking that our happiness is up there on the top of the mountain . . . but what if it's not?

Following are five ways we commonly see people exhibit a fear of success. As you read through this list, look deep down inside and ask yourself whether any of them sound true to you. Pay special attention to the reasons you deny especially hard! Are you trying to prove anything to yourself or to others?

Reason 1: "If I achieve that goal I won't be who I am. I'll change somehow and my friends won't like me anymore."

Very often people are afraid that if they reach their goal they will have to stop being who they are and start playing someone else's role. Do you think that in order to become successful someone is asking you to turn into an evil, bloodthirsty monster? You can be a wonderful person, both spiritually and materially wealthy, and remain true to yourself and well liked by others who are important to you.

You will have to change to be successful. You read this right. Read it again. Underline it. Remember it. You cannot achieve great new things without changing who you are and what you do. But this doesn't mean that it has to be a change for the worse.

Don't let change scare you. Life is a constant motion, a constant change. It throws down a challenge to change or get left behind. This keeps us growing, moving forward, and getting rid of the obstacles that slow us down.

Success is often tied to all kinds of limiting and unrealistic beliefs that have been pounded into our minds by others. But the fact is that achievement is something that is very good indeed. In all honesty, do you want your kids (nieces, nephews, friends) to be successes or failures? Then why not yourself?

Reason 2: "I'm not worth it. I don't deserve to be successful."

This type of fear of success is a big source of self-sabotage. First of all, you have to be honest enough with yourself to admit if you do have a challenge with your self-worth. Can you admit that you think you don't deserve to be successful? Most of the time, people aren't that honest with themselves. Self-deception is the easiest form of deception there is!

People hide the true reason for their self-doubt behind many little, unimportant reasons, and the feeling that "I am not worthy!" is hiding behind closed doors. You can't treat the cause if you can't find it. Being straight with yourself is one of the most important factors of achieving anything important in life.

There are many other reasons for a fear of success caused by a negative self-image. One of them is a lack of belief in your own ability to sustain progress and maintain the accomplishments you have achieved in your life. Sometimes you think, "Wow, I think I just got totally lucky."

Another is the belief that there are others out there who are better and smarter than you, who will replace or displace you. We won't argue with you on this. You are right! There are people better and smarter than you and there always will be. But there are also millions of people who don't hold a candle to you! Do what you need to do to see that you *are* worthy of the success you desire.

Reason 3: "It is impossible!"

What can you do if you don't believe it is possible? *Believe.* Say to yourself (or better yet, out loud and with emotion): *"If someone else has done it, so can I!"*

Someone else has already done almost everything on this planet at one time or another. There probably are many cases similar to yours if you look. And there are countless examples of accomplishments that were considered impossible before somebody did them. No one ran a sub-four-minute mile until . . . someone did. No one climbed Mount Everest . . . until someone did. After the first person accomplished these things (and made them "possible"), many others quickly followed. Achievement isn't rocket science. Analyze what you have to do to achieve your goal. What do you have in common with the person who has already achieved a goal similar to yours? What else do you need to have or need to change about yourself? What obstacles are in your way and how can you overcome them? Once you do all that, consider 80 percent of your job to be done.

The key to your success is following someone else's example while making your contribution unique. People use the same interstate highways everyday to get to different places. You just have to free that great thinker, great winner, and great fighter.

Realize that this is not a question of the actual possibility or impossibility of your goal. It is your personal belief. Find people who disagree with this belief and have done what you think is impossible. Then reframe your goal as possible and get ready for the challenge of achieving it.

Reason 4: "I can't do it!"

Kids love this excuse. Remember when a task didn't really sound appealing to you (like your math homework or making your own breakfast), and you pulled out that "I can't do it" excuse? Usually this meant, "I don't know how to do it." Sometimes it meant, "This requires too much effort or practice to get good at it."

And most of the time this excuse worked for you! Someone would help you solve the math problem or would cook your breakfast for you. Today? Are you still using the same excuse, hoping that some other person will do all the hard work for you? Ouch.

"I can't do it!" results from a lack of knowledge or ability. That problem is easily fixed. You can gain the knowledge and teach yourself how to do whatever it is you need to do. It is quite simple really. Unfortunately most people don't look at it that way. They see their inability as some sort of sign: "If I can't do it, it is not meant to be."

Think about what would happen if, for a day, you believed that you *can* do something as strongly as you believed you can't? Really ponder this. You probably will see that this would be enough to get you over the hump and get the job done.

Reason 5: "The goal is not worth my effort."

What if the goal does not sound exciting to you?

For example, you know enough about computers to find a good job. You can learn more in this area and even expect to get a raise and a better position. It will take about three years of your life, but you know you can get there. You know you will be making over $120,000 a year; you will have a nice car and a nice house.

The problem is that you hate the idea of spending most of your day in the stuffy office, sitting in front of the computer screen. You hate the idea of not being able to spend any time with your family, but for their sake you are ready to do it.

What should you do? This is a bit of a trick question. When it feels like a goal simply is not worth your effort, there may be a simple alternative. Go back to the drawing board to find another goal that is both worth your effort and will make you happy. Why waste years of your life doing something you don't like, when you could be doing something that you enjoy or you find rewarding or heaven forbid, both?

Success Actions That Work: Have you been struggling with any of these ways of fearing success? Take action to remove them from your life. Sure, everyone has a fear of something. Terrorists and flesh-eating bacteria are scary. But there's no reason to fear the good stuff.

Use your fears as a valuable tool for awareness. This is a benefit of fear. It can be a beacon to reveal your limiting beliefs.

Any fear (besides those that reflect genuine dangers, of course) can tell you something about yourself. Where fear lives, so do limiting beliefs. Learn to use this knowledge to your advantage. Follow your fears directly to the roots of your limiting beliefs, and begin work on eliminating them. Use the fear generated by reaching for success to further propel yourself forward.

Question: **What is the most effective way to introduce success principles to get kids on the right track in life?**

Each of the authors of this book has kids and feels strongly about introducing them to the principles in this book. We share some ideas and differ on others. Dave is going to answer this question as the father of a three-year-old and Mollie is going to answer it as the mother of three children, ages eight, ten, and thirteen.

Dave

I have a three-year-old daughter at the writing of this book, and I spend a great deal of time thinking about these things. I'm confident that many of the examples we set for our children when they are very young and many of the experiences we create for them are the things they often learn for life. With that in mind I constantly look for ways of expanding experiences, teaching positive lessons, and avoiding the bad lessons that many adults are wont to give. Let me give you an example.

When my daughter was two years old we were camping with family and friends over a holiday. My daughter, who I was observing, decided to walk into the dark woods. So I quietly followed a safe distance behind to observe what she would do and, of course, to be sure that she didn't hurt herself. While we were walking another adult slipped up to me and said, "I'm going to walk down the hill on the other side and when she gets near me I'm going to

jump out and scare her so she won't walk off in the dark again."
I was beside myself and told that individual in no uncertain terms
that if he did that I'd drag him into the woods and leave permanent psychological scars and I meant it! He walked away and my
daughter continued a little further in the woods and sat down on
a rock. After a while I walked up to her and asked what she was
doing and she said looking at the moon. She simply wanted to be
away from the fire where it was hard to see the moon and be in a
place where she could easily see it.

If I had let the misguided individual scare my daughter, there
were many possible outcomes, none of which I could see as being
positive. My daughter who still isn't scared of the dark could have
developed a fear of the dark. She could have developed a dislike
for the forest. She could have developed an unhealthy distrust of
people, and the list goes on.

I used the opportunity to speak with her and tell her about
being safe at night. We picked a walking stick so she could poke
where she couldn't see, and we talked about always letting mom
and dad know where she was going. All had much more positive
outcomes than the plan of my well meaning friend.

The way to teach children success principles is to set up situations where they can succeed. Help them solve problems and
celebrate like mad when they do. Encourage them to find solutions on their own and to revel in the joy of attaining goals.
Tell them the truth about competition. In every game there are
winners and losers as in business, politics, love, and life. Let them
experience the joy of winning. Create opportunities for them to
experience things you never did at their age even if they are simple things. Introduce them to ethnic food early on. Take them to
cultural festivals. Have them start learning a second language at an
early age.

Build self-esteem. I have never told my daughter that anything
was impossible; I let her discover her limitations on her own, and I

help her learn how to overcome them. Praise them appropriately. Saying they are smart when they are not doesn't make them smart or build esteem. Showing them how to accomplish something and praising them for their mastery does. Complimenting them on specific behaviors they do well encourages repetition. Allow them to fail, allow them to take risks. Encourage risk-taking early (use sense and be safe), and reward them for being willing to do something that other kids find fearful. Value things like reading, learning, and education and teach them to value these things as well. Also, teach them how to value life experience.

Teach them the value of hard work early; a strong work ethic is learned by doing not by observing. Teach them about following through on their commitments by following through on your own. You are the best teacher they'll ever have.

Talk to them and teach them about success early and often. Teach them the value of money and how money works, if you still don't know find someone who does so that they learn early on.

Most of all, be present with them as they learn. Be curious with them, explore with them, and celebrate with them. When you are present and in the moment with them you are creating a memory that will serve as an example for a lifetime. Those are the moments that matter.

Encourage them to explore and challenge and not accept "because I said so" as an answer. Eliminate that phrase from your vocabulary and support them when they challenge other adults who use it or some equally disempowering phrase. Teach them determination and reward them for demonstrating it. Allow them to be stubborn in their beliefs sometimes. Lead them to the right conclusion through experience not through telling.

Finally, teach them to give and to receive. Not just gifts and money, but praise and appreciation. You can't start too early. If you lay a foundation for success in your children, teach them to create their own success, to learn to take risks, to value exploration, education, and experience, you'll give them a foundation most of us never had.

And, never forget to show them how much you love them, always, in good times or bad, in public and in private. Being loved helps children learn to love themselves and others.

Never forget the biggest influence children have in their early years is you. What you do for yourself, what you demonstrate through your actions is setting the course for your child's future. If that isn't the encouragement you need to get up every day and push yourself a little harder, to experience a little more, and to accomplish one more thing, then you need to take a long look at where you are and where you're going with your life. Let your life be the example that they always use as their beacon of truth.

Mollie

I have taught child psychology courses in personality and social development. But this answer comes more from my experience as a mother. A large part of my personal definition of success is to be the best mother I can be to my children. I take seriously both living the success principles as a role model to my children and teaching them these principles as life tools. Kids watch what you do, not what you say. If you want to raise successful children, walk your talk. Be authentic. Be consistent.

One of the most important steps in introducing success principles to your children is to *listen* to them. Chunk your time so that when you are with your kids, you are fully there and not just in body. Give them your full attention. Be present in each moment with them. These complete moments will lead to deep connections, meaningful talks, new discoveries, and joyful parenting. These moments will make memories for your children that will last a lifetime. It is the experiences that come from these seemingly mundane and inconsequential moments that will lay the foundation for their success (and will be talked about at your funeral.)

Integrate an ongoing discussion about ethical and success principles into your relationship with your children. This is important to do with any issues that can affect the rest of their lives. Engaged parents do not believe in such a thing as "the talk." Any important issue requires a discussion that begins when your child is young and continues over time, taking into consideration their physical, intellectual, and emotional maturity along the way.

Give your children opportunities to use the success principles and develop skills. Give them chores to teach them self-discipline. Give them projects and oversee that they carry them through to completion. Help them create a habit of finishing things. Use a chore structure to teach about money and wealth building. Our two oldest kids already follow the stock market, learn about entrepreneurship, seek out opportunities to earn money, and understand the power of compound interest. We teach our kids about the duty and joys of sharing and they divide their allowance and chore money into thirds (long-term save, short-term save/spend, and give). Volunteer together as a family.

Show your children that you value a well-rounded education, including book learning, travel, and life experience. Encourage them to ask questions, explore, use critical thinking skills, and find their own answers. Support them in taking calculated risks, handling setbacks, and celebrating successes. Teach them to focus on the process of learning and growing and not solely on the results produced.

Ask your children about their dreams and record these for them to look back upon if they should lose their way as adults. As they get older, encourage them to journal. Continuously broaden your children's world in alignment with their unique interests and give them choices. We support our children in playing musical instruments and learning second languages. They choose the instruments and the languages. We cherish the moments when we see our kids' eyes light up as they experience something for the first time. What a thrill when we can say, "Today, your world just got a little bigger."

Love your children unconditionally. Let them see your eyes light up when they walk into the room because you are happy that they are in your life. Love them through their good choices and bad, through their victories and shortcomings. Let your love serve as an anchor for your children as they grow and go out into this world to create their own success.

Parenting can be challenging. Remember to celebrate your successes along the way! When you have a clear understanding of the type of parent you want to be, these moments take on a deeper significance. I remember an open house at school when our oldest child was in kindergarten. On one wall, the kids had been given a sheet a paper with the outline of a house and underneath a sentence read, "My house is a place where _____." I scanned the various houses where kids had drawn pictures of themselves doing something and written activities like "I eat," "I sleep," and "I play." My son's picture was on the very bottom row. His read, "My house is a place where I am loved," and he had drawn a picture of our family standing in our home holding hands. This was a moment that deeply touched my heart and confirmed to me that my husband and I were on the right path in raising a child who would succeed in life.

As a parent, you can never throw up your hands in surrender. You don't give up on your kids. This simply is not an option. As your children age and you experience less direct influence on them, continue to direct their choice of friends and how they spend their time. No matter what the challenges of any particular child, you can create opportunities for them to make good choices and then catch them doing good. Point out their small victories. Reward them. Celebrate their progress with them.

The bottom line of success parenting is *you do what it takes* to support your child's independence and success. Kids do not come with any guarantees. For example, our youngest child didn't speak for a couple years, so we learned sign language and got her the professional support she needed. She now is in a regular classroom and continuing to make great strides. Our middle child had a brain injury at six months of age, followed by a year of seizures. She now is thriving. Last year, our oldest child asked to be home schooled. Although we had never entertained the idea of home schooling, it became clear that he simply needed more. We actively searched for the solutions that would meet his needs. He is now dual enrolled, taking some advanced classes at school and doing a series of independent study projects at home.

Each child is unique and each family comes with its own set of parenting challenges. For me, success parenting is about taking each individual child as they are, giving them the skills and resources they need to realize their full potential, and trying to enjoy each moment with them along the way.

Question: I hear success gurus say, "If you can dream it, you can achieve it." This sounds like an oversimplification. Or do you agree with this statement?

A statement that, "All you have to do is dream it and you can achieve it," would be a gross oversimplification. Having read this far, you know that achieving at a high level requires self-discipline and effort. It requires directed action. Implementation is key. So obviously, you need to do much more than just dream.

But we do agree that with the right tools, people can achieve nearly any dream. Success minds believe in the power of dreams. Even more important, success minds focus on the "how to" and not on any so-called impossibility. People who achieve at a high level refuse to focus on and give energy to why things can't be done. Rather, they get busy thinking about how they can do things.

Many people allow perceived or false limitations to hold them back from achieving their dreams. But you are not one of those people are you? You are someone who, after reading this book, wants more. You are driven to have more. Sure, maybe you've tried in the past and it didn't work. Maybe you've failed and had setbacks, maybe you are not in a great place right at this moment. Maybe money is tight or your family is reluctant to support your efforts. Maybe you are just plain afraid to try. Big deal, it isn't the end of the world. Hold on to your dreams.

Success Actions That Work: Do this exercise now to help develop your success mind. Write down a complete list of things that you want to accomplish in life (you might want to look back at the list of dreams you created if you did the exercise in Chapter 5.) Include how you want to spend your time, where you want to go, and what you want to accomplish.

Now, write down all of the reasons you will not be able to achieve them. Write down all of the reasons you will fail. Write down all of the things that people will say or what you think they will say (trust us, you imagine them thinking about your failures much more than they actually think about them.) Write down every reason why you cannot accomplish your dream. Be thorough. Don't leave any nagging thought or negative idea out. Put it all down on paper.

Then ask yourself, "What would happen if I did achieve my dream?" Write down your answers.

Finally, ask yourself these two questions: What is the very worst thing that could happen if I try? And if that happened, what would I do? Write down your answers.

Now that you have gained some perspective, go back to the list of negative factors that could hold you back from achieving your dreams. Take each item one at a time and honestly assess whether it is in fact a hurdle to your achievement. If not, cross it off. If it is a real challenge, ask yourself, "How could I change the outcome?"

Let's look at an example. Say your dream is to solve the problem of homelessness in your town. You ask yourself what factors could keep you from succeeding at this.

Answer: People will say it is impossible, my friends will question why I would try, it will cost a lot of money, I might fail, I don't know what government regulations would stop my efforts.

You then turn to solution generation with the question, "How?" Ask yourself how you could change the outcomes.

How could I make people see it is possible? How can I get my friends to see that this is a worthwhile opportunity? How can I raise the money necessary? How can I be sure I won't fail? How can I find out what government regulations exist around private solutions to homelessness?

Here are some possible answers to a couple of these questions:

How could I make people see it is possible?

I could end homelessness for one person and one family and demonstrate how anyone could do the same thing. I could document the model and give it to a hundred people who are interested in helping the homeless and get them to do the same thing so we have a bigger case study. I could invite the media to watch as I end homelessness for one person. I could invite members of my church to see how it is done so that they could tell more people. I could invite teenagers doing their Eagle Scout projects to consider doing this as their project so that the Boy Scouts of America could see how it could make a massive difference across the country. I could get the company that does bus bench advertising to give me space on all its benches for messages for one week. I could put flyers on every car at Wal-Mart.

How can I raise the money necessary?

I can get a philanthropist to donate the necessary money. I can apply for grants. I can go to every church in town and tell them what I'm doing and ask them to let me explain my project and take a special offering for me. I can ask every business in my town to donate 10 dollars to my cause. I can get children to gather money at school to help by showing them how their pennies can make a difference. I can document my project on the Internet and ask for donations. I can get a local video company or TV crew to document what I'm doing and tell the stories of the homeless people I'm helping. I can get a local movie theater to let me do a special showing where people can pay a higher fee to attend. I can ask a celebrity and a restaurant to support me and sell tickets to have dinner with the celebrity. I can take money out of my savings to get started.

What ways can you think of that we didn't list here to answer the questions above? There are many!

See what happens when you start thinking about the how and not the why something won't work? You get wildly creative and come up with many solutions for what first appeared to be impossible.

Use this same process to help achieve your dreams. What would happen if you decided to start the business you've always dreamed of? What would happen if you didn't care what anyone thought? What would happen if this time you just did it?

How are you going to do these things? We know that you can because dreams are rarely impossible. You simply have not considered all of the possible solutions.

References

Armstrong, Lance, and Sally Jenkins. 2000. *It's Not About the Bike*. New York: Putnam.

Buzan, Tony. 2002. *Head First*. New York: Thorsons (an imprint of HarperCollins).

Deutschman, Alan. 2007. *Change or Die*. New York: HarperCollins.

Ferriss, Tim. 2007. *The 4-Hour Workweek*. New York: Crown.

Frankl, Victor. 1985. *Man's Search for Meaning*. New York: Washington Square Press.

Hill, Napoleon. 1963. *Think and Grow Rich*. New York: Random House.

Lakhani, David. 2006. *The Power of an Hour*. Hoboken, NJ: John Wiley & Sons.

Osborn, Alex. 1979. *Applied Imagination: Principals and Procedures of Creative Thinking*. New York: Charles Scribner's Sons.

Peale, Norman Vincent. 2007. *The Power of Positive Thinking*. New York: Fireside Publishing.

Seligman, Martin E. P. 2006. *Learned Optimism*. New York: Vintage Publishing.

Resources

Here Are Your Two Free Tickets to Success Factors Live

Success is a habit and habits are created through powerful experiences and positive repetition. We want this to be the most valuable book you have ever read. To make this happen, we would like to give you two free tickets to our breakthrough success event called Success Factors Live.

Success Factors Live is a life and business success mastery program designed to help you experience your full potential. For a limited time, the $1,497 attendance price is waived for you if you own the book. To get your free tickets simply follow the instructions below.

Unlike many success events this is not a rah-rah motivational event that leaves you feeling pumped up for a short while. Success Factors Live is a carefully crafted experiential event designed to help you learn and integrate the most important success factors into your life and into your business.

When you attend Success Factors Live you'll begin developing the solid foundations of success habits that last a lifetime. This event is orchestrated and lead by the authors for the most profound experience available. We'll also have surprise special guests who will take your learning deeper than you've ever imagined possible. You'll be learning, implementing, connecting, and succeeding in ways you've never before experienced.

Here's how you register: Simply go to www.bestsuccessfactors. com and click on the link that says Success Factors Live. We will be running the event across the country for a limited time so be sure to register today as seats will be filled on a first–registered, first-served basis. You will need to bring this book with you in addition to registering to get in. If you want to bring your team, simply buy them books and register them with you! Visit www. bestsuccessfactors.com to register and see a complete explanation of what you'll be learning in this exciting success immersion.

We look forward to training you and to helping you develop a plan that will transform your business and your life!

About the
Authors

Kevin Hogan holds a doctorate in psychology and is the author of 18 books, including *The Secret Language of Business, Selling: Powerful New Strategies for Sales Success, Covert Persuasion, The Science of Influence, The Psychology of Persuasion, Talk Your Way to the Top, Irresistible Attraction, Covert Hypnosis,* and *The New Hypnotherapy Handbook.*

He is body language expert and unconscious influence expert to the BBC, the *New York Post* and dozens of popular magazines like *In Touch, First for Women, Success!,* and *Cosmopolitan.* He has become the go-to resource for analyzing key White House figures. Hogan has taught Persuasion and Influence at the University of St. Thomas Management Center and is a frequent media guest. Articles by and about him have appeared in *Success!, Redbook, Office Pro, Selling Power, Cosmopolitan, Maxim, Playboy,* and numerous other publications. He was recently featured in a half dozen magazines (including *wProst*) in Poland after teaching persuasion and influence skills to that country's 350 leading sales managers.

Kevin Hogan is generally agreed to be the nation's leading body language expert. Kevin is a dynamic, well-known international public speaker, consultant, and corporate trainer. He has taught persuasion, sales, and marketing skills to leaders in the government of Poland, employees from Boeing, Microsoft, Starbucks, Cargill, Pillsbury, Carlson Companies, Fortis Insurance, Great Clips, the State of Minnesota, 3M, the United States Postal Service, and numerous other Fortune 500 companies. He recently spoke to The Inner Circle and at the Million Dollar Roundtable convention in Las Vegas.

Kevin's keynotes, seminars, and workshops help companies sell, market, and communicate more effectively. His cutting-edge research into the mind and keen understanding of consumer behavior create a unique distillation of information never before released to the public. Each customized program he leads is fit specifically to the needs of the group or organization. Kevin gives his audiences new and easy to implement ideas to achieve excellence.

Dave Lakhani is the President of Bold Approach, Inc., the nation's first business acceleration strategy firm. A business acceleration strategy firm is a company that helps companies seduce consumers, build relationships, dominate top of mind awareness, and create powerful personal and company brands . . . *fast*.

Dave has been responsible for developing dynamic strategies driving record-breaking growth and increases in sales in more than 500 businesses in the past 10 years. Dave is an in-demand speaker, author, and trainer, whose ideas have been applied by some of the biggest organizations in the United States including IBM, the U.S. Army, Rogers Media, Micron, GE, Wizard Academy, and many more. Dave's advice is frequently seen in magazines including *Selling Power, Sales and Marketing Management, Entrepreneur, Business Solutions, Retail Systems Reseller, Integrated Solutions, Home Office Computing, PC Magazine*, and other media including *Business Radio*

Network, The Business Connection, The Today Show, and dozens more. He has been featured in more than 50 books.

Dave's company, Bold Approach, Inc., was nominated as one of *Fast Company* magazine's Fast 50 companies and Dave was runner-up for the 2007 American Business Award For America's Best Sales Trainer.

Visit Dave at www.boldapproach.com, www.howtopersuade. com, or www.powerofanhour.com.

Dave is the author of: *Persuasion—The Art of Getting What You Want, The Power of an Hour—Business and Life Mastery in One Hour a Week, Subliminal Persuasion—Influence and Marketing Secrets They Don't Want You to Know,* and *Making Marketing Work* (audiobook).

Mollie Marti, Ph.D., J.D., is a psychologist who specializes in performance in competitive environments. She is an Adjunct Professor of Psychology at the University of Iowa and is widely published in academic journals of psychology and human behavior. She is also author of *Selling: Powerful New Strategies for Sales Success.* As an active researcher and consultant, her knowledge of motivation and performance effectiveness puts her on the cutting edge of performance issues. She provides unique value to corporate clients by motivating their workforce and creating effective selling, marketing, business, and leadership strategies to accelerate growth, improve productivity, and increase profits.

As a performance coach, Mollie shares tools and lessons from her rich and varied experience as a psychologist, lawyer, mediator, performance coach, successful entrepreneur, working mother, and more. As a trainer and speaker, she combines a rich personal history of motivating and leading teams to success with a genuine passion for empowering others to live fulfilling and successful lives. She speaks from a place of deep conviction and a lifetime of accomplishments as she trains organizations in leadership, sales, team building, business strategy, conflict resolution, life balance, and self-mastery skills. She delivers real-world wisdom and scientific research coupled with inspirational stories and humor in a way that moves and motivates audiences to produce lasting results.

Mollie lives on an apple orchard in Mount Vernon, Iowa, with her husband Monte, their three children, two naughty yellow labs, a large family of cats, and various other pets. She is a health and fitness enthusiast who enjoys adventures with family, travel, wine tasting, reading, and cruising in her Volkswagen bug convertible. Visit her online at www.molliemarti.com.

Index

jobs *vs.*, 137, 139–141
 risk taking and, 139–141, 147–148
 time management and, 148–152
Workplace, 129–134. *See also* Colleagues;
 Jobs; Work spaces

Work spaces, 42–43
Writing. *See* Journaling; Lists

Yes, power of, 186–189. *See also*
 Affirmations